The Lympstone Story

*A revised and updated edition with
extra chapters and much new material*

Edited by Rosemary Smith

The Lympstone Society

2005

The red cliffs of Lyonstone

The Lympstone Story

GEOLOGY

The Red Cliffs of Lympstone

The eastern shore of the Exe Estuary has steeper slopes than the more marshy west side, and at Lympstone red cliffs face the water. Darling's Rock, just north of the harbour, was an important marker for the boundary of the Manor of Kenton, which ran southward to the Checkstone in the sea off Exmouth. The rock used to be much larger - it is said sheep grazed upon it - but erosion has reduced its size, just as the cliffs themselves have been worn back. A few years ago concern was expressed about the falling cliffs and the National Trust was worried that there might be legal liability if anyone should suffer injury from falling over the edge. I examined the cliffs and concluded that there was no exceptional danger of future cliff falls, but that a small cave in gravel close to the harbour should be made safe. Safety is important: anyone looking at the cliffs should take care not to dislodge any pebbles from the top, and not to stand underneath when others are doing so.

Mention of gravel brings up the question of what the cliffs are made of: ask anybody and they will reply "red sandstone", but that is only partly true. In fact they are made mainly of red breccia, a gravelly rock laid down by floods many million years ago, with only thin sandstone strata within them. The grey gravels at the top of the cliffs are river terraces formed just thousands of years ago when the River Exe - and the sea into which it ran - was at a higher level than today, at least 30 feet higher. Further north along the estuary, river terraces have yielded stone tools, evidence of human occupation from those ancient times: so the earliest Lympstonians may have lived on a gravel flat beside a wider river with no red cliffs, catching fish and hunting wild animals in the forests of Woodbury and Exton!

But the red rocks are the most interesting, because they record a time, more than 250 million years ago, when the terrain was like a sub-tropical desert and there was a large mountain range where Dartmoor now is. Rain fell only rarely but came as violent storms when it did: rocks, gravel and sand from the desert mountains cascaded down into the adjacent valleys, to be deposited as alluvial fans across wide desert plains. As layer built upon layer, and the hot semi-arid climate weathered the material to a red colour - much like northern Nigeria at the present day - so huge fans of gravel formed and sand dunes blew up onto them. Today we find the dunes mainly in the red cliffs of Dawlish, with gravelly fan deposits below and above. The latter, named the Langstone Breccias, form the Lympstone cliffs and give evidence that uplift of the mountain ranges caused gravel deposition to reach Lympstone again.

Looking at the breccia strata, one can find abundant fragments of hard grey sandstone (Culm) and black rocks from the margin of the Dartmoor granite: they must therefore have come from an area dominated by such rocks. Observing the flow directions in the strata shows that they originated as a fan starting in the vicinity of Doddiscombsleigh, where Culm sandstones are very common. At Lympstone, however, the breccias are much less coarse than on the west side of the river, which means that here we have only the outer fringe of the gravel fan. These are best seen at Sowden End, and the top of the cliff shows a transition to sandstone and mudstone strata, more easily seen in the cliffs at Exmouth.

Although I have looked long and hard, no fossils have been reported from Lympstone. At Exmouth a few worm tubes and plant fragments have been found, and some primitive reptile bones in the cliffs east of Budleigh Salterton. (Now known as the Jurassic Coast. Ed.)

Inland, although layers of red or buff sandstone can be found - one such layer just south of the mill was quarried in the 15th century to build the church - most of the land is underlain by red mudstone or marl. As many gardeners know, the soil also has many extremely hard pebbles: these were washed down into the soil of Lympstone and elsewhere during the Ice Ages when the local landscape was a barren arctic wasteland, before the native forests reappeared. These spade-resistant garden obstacles come from the Budleigh Salterton Pebble Beds, probably about 220 million years old, which today form the ridge of Woodbury Common but once extended further west. These were laid down by a great river that flowed across from France before the English Channel was created. When that river stopped flowing, a sandy desert formed instead, depositing a thick layer of red sand known as the Otter Sandstone. This spread eastwards into Dorset, and a large oilfield has been found by drilling into it near Swanage. But the chances of an oil gusher in Lympstone are very remote indeed!

Dr. D.J.C. Laming

GEOGRAPHY

Geographical Continuity and Change

Lympstone nestles between two low New Red Sandstone cliffs on the east shore of the Exe estuary from which the village runs inland along the valley of the Watton Brook. The estuarine railway line from Exmouth to Exeter divides the harbour and fishing cottages of Lower Lympstone from the parish church and the upper village, while the agricultural land and farms of the parish extend east up to the heights of Lympstone and Woodbury Commons at about 500 feet. Lympstone is thus a 'strip parish' characteristic of many in East Devon which provided in times past a share of many different resources - from the stony woodlands and heathlands of the commons, the mixed sandy and clay soils of the middle parish, the lush meadows of the lower Watton Brook, and, of course, the fisheries of the estuary and beyond. Those who lived in Lympstone in the centuries before us found themselves fortunately situated by comparison with those far inland; most of those who live here today recognise that they are equally favoured.

Let's imagine that Colonel Thomas Hussey who lived in Highcliffe House a hundred years ago could take a walk up through the village seeing into the future to our present day. In some senses he might feel quite at home. He would pass under the then new railway bridge and along the narrow highway of what we call Strand and Church Road, tarmac now, roughly metalled then, but still narrow and lined with cottages, "Georgian" and Victorian villas then as now. Past the village school, built in 1823 and extended at the end of his century to take 220 pupils, next the parish church, then tidy after its major nineteenth-century restoration and extension; now similarly neat with a new roof of Welsh slates. No polythene-covered greenhouses then to interrupt Colonel Hussey's view from the churchyard across the meadows to the parish water mill and the hamlet of Sowden, new also would be the twentieth-century housing infill along Longmeadow Road but, by and large, it would seem a familiar scene, then as now. So, on across the

An aerial view of Lympstone

Exmouth to Exeter main road and up Watton Lane to the top of the parish. Were he to visit his friend Harry Landon at Tedstone House and take in the present-day view from the high windows up to the Common in the east, he would still feel fairly comfortable. The fields of today would look much bigger to him, more grass than in his time, a few new houses, but the same scrubby woodland, albeit with fewer conifers, on the skyline. But if he chose a window looking back over Lympstone, his impression of stability would be rocked by the shock of change. Though many of the buildings of 'his' Lympstone still grace its central street, away from this there is much that is new, while the kinds of people who live here and the ways in which they earn their livings are quite literally a world apart from a century and a half ago.

There are more people now. 150 years ago there were just a thousand inhabitants, and the number remained more or less the same at every census until the Second World War. Much of the increase to the 2001 census figure of 1,884 has occurred in the last forty years. Colonel Hussey would be struck by the orderly rows of a small local authority housing estate above the church and the houses built for personnel employed at Royal Marine Commando, Lympstone. Away on the other side of the Watton valley, he would see the private housing estate built in the grounds of his then neighbour, Frank Pearce, of Underhill House. Here and there he would see other new houses, some in small groups, as along Greenhill Avenue and Strawberry Hill, others in ones and twos infilling between buildings he would have known well.

What of the people? Farming has never been the major source of employment in Lympstone; there were always more involved in fishing and lace making than working the land. In the mid-nineteenth century, the parish tithe survey tells us that there were about a dozen small farms of 25-60 acres. Colonel Hussey would recognise the farm names of today: Potters, Wootton and Sowden, though he would look in vain for the ancient rectorial manor of Lympstone, now dispersed. Gone also are most of the 92 acres of orchards; Long Orchard, Old Orchard and like names are clues as to where they once were. Farmers no longer devote a quarter of their land to growing turnips; the large flocks of sheep that fed off them and helped fertilise the soil are likewise only a memory. There are still horses and ponies but not the eighty working horses recorded in 1839. By contrast, any visitor from the past would be amazed at the number of dairy cows today and the small proportion of land under arable and market garden crops. But the land is still farmed; lace making is kept alive only as a heritage craft, fishing (*described separately, see page 37*) has all but gone. Colonel Hussey would be amazed to read that in 1989 the Lympstone Village Appraisal found that about a quarter of Lympstone's population is retired, that the school has not many more than a hundred pupils, and that of those in paid employment, almost three-quarters commute to work elsewhere, many to Exeter. Perhaps even more bizarre to a visitor from the past is that quite a few of the smaller cottages are no longer permanently occupied but are enjoyed for holidays and as rural retreats by visitors from many miles away. From fishing and farming and Honiton lace to a retirement and 'dormitory' and holiday village; the social and economic world of Lympstone has changed!

Why don't you retrace Colonel Hussey's walk? Tedstone House is not open to you but if you make your way on up towards Lympstone Common, you can enjoy a similar view.

Professor Roger J.P. Kain, F.B.A.,
Deputy Vice Chancellor, Exeter University

ARCHAEOLOGY

Excavation and Findings, 2003

We, Charlotte Coles and Barry Russell, undertook an archaeological excavation in Lympstone in the summer of 2003, to discover more about the history of the area. The excavation took place opposite the church, in the field once known as "Front Meadow"; this field also used to contain a house and garden known as "Fowlers".

A large amount of research was done into Lympstone and the site before the excavation was started. Research showed that three Bronze Age round barrows are located on Lympstone Common, near Fryingpans. These barrows are in line east-west, are covered in bracken and are easier to see when the bracken has died down (SY031 850). A Roman coin has also been found in the village; other than that very little archaeology has been undertaken in Lympstone.

Before excavating we checked that the site was not a Scheduled Ancient Monument (S.A.M.) by ringing up the Devon County Council's Archaeology Unit, as excavating a S.A.M. without permission from the government is against the law. After finding out that it was not a S.A.M., we looked at the Tithe Map of 1839 for the area, which showed "Fowlers". We researched aerial photography for Lympstone at the National Monuments Records in Swindon, however nothing striking showed up on them. We also looked at the census, documents etc. to find out more about the family history and what kind of people lived in "Fowlers".

Firstly a check with the Tithe Map shows a Catherine Wright living in her own house and garden: this was confirmed with the 1841 census a few years later as Catherine Wright, widow, living with an Emily Wright (both of independent means) accompanied by two female servants. This was obviously turning out to be a family of some wealth. A quick tour of the inside of the church uncovered a plaque dedicated to Catherine Jane Wright, died 1844, wife of John Thomas Wright who died in 1838. Using the computer's Familysearch (I.G.I.) website, a marriage of John Thomas Wright and Catherine Jane Northcote, 26th August, 1782 at Ottery St. Mary, was discovered. We know for sure this was the right couple for our Lympstone site. A further trip to the West Country Studies Library and the Devon Record Office, Exeter, revealed that our John Thomas Wright had been elected Mayor of Exeter in 1805, and that Catherine's family, the Northcotes, had a family seat at Upton Pyne, with her father being the sixth baronet. The name of the property opposite the church at Lympstone was found in the 1832 Election Rolls as "Fowlers", being given as in the ownership of John T. Wright. So now we have a continuing picture of a family of some means living in a prominent location opposite the church, a family of which everyone in the village would know. Their son, Captain William Henry Wright went on to have Lympstone House built, having owned much of the surrounding land. With his death in 1867, leaving £7,000 in his will, a window behind the Lady Chapel's altar was devoted to William, finally making the very public statement of the importance of this family in their time.

After this research had been completed, digging could start. Two small trenches were dug; the first was located to explore a slightly raised mound which had previously been hard to plough through; it was also between two fences on the Tithe Map. The second trench, 1.30m x 0.60m, was located to try to find any remaining foundations or building materials from the house.

Conditions were hard and it was exceptionally hot and sunny and this baked the soil. The layers of soil had to be identified and recorded. Our activities received a lot of attention from passers-by and villagers who stopped and asked us if we were digging for oil or extending the churchyard!

The finds came in thick and fast and 605 finds were located in one 2m x 1m trench alone. Most of these finds were associated with the occupation of the house, objects such as glass, animal bones (including pig, sheep, cow and cat bones); slate and shells were very common finds, and a huge number of clay pipe stems were found as well. A large amount of Medieval and Post-Medieval pottery was found, including a rim of a Victorian chamberpot and part of a cooking pot still with the soot on the side, where it had been placed over a fire. A fair few pieces of the Post-Medieval pottery came from abroad, including four pieces of pottery from the Low Countries known as Westerwald; this pottery is highly glazed and coloured grey and bright blue. The pieces we found were from a tankard. Another piece of foreign pottery was a piece of 'Bellarmine' jug. This jug was also made in the same area in the 17th and 18th centuries. These huge jugs had the face of an old man stuck on the neck and as time went by the faces were made more and more grumpy! The only coin found during the excavation was a token from 1660, the time of the Commonwealth, from Ottery St. Mary and was minted by a merchant called Thomas Osmond. Another find from the time of the Civil War was that of a lead top to a gunpowder flask. During the Civil War, Lympstone was held by the Parliamentarians.

However, as we dug deeper in the trenches, rarer and older finds began to surface. Nine sherds of late Saxon/early Norman pottery (C11th-12th) were discovered, two of particularly higher quality. Two pieces of late Bronze Age/early Iron Age pottery were also found.

Nevertheless the pieces of flint were the star finds and certainly a great surprise for us. Sixteen pieces were found in total both from the Mesolithic period (10,000-6,000 B.C.) and the Neolithic period (6,000-2,600 B.C.). Three flint knives were found and have been beautifully made. A layer of cobbles was also found in one trench possibly from a fallen-down wall or part of an old walkway. Bill Horner, Devon County Archaeologist came to see that they weren't important, then we had to draw them. The finds were taken to John Allan, then Curator of Antiquities at Exeter Museum, to be identified and dated. They then had to be properly recorded, which includes being given a number, measured, drawn and photographed. This kept me very busy as the final total was over 800.

We felt that our findings were too good to be kept to ourselves and so many people had been interested in our excavation that we decided to have an open day to show what we had been up to. It was a big success and many people came. Two groups of school children also came to look at the dig, and seemed very interested.

The excavation showed that Lympstone is considerably older than originally thought. Further excavations are planned and the full report for 2003 is in the Devon County Council Sites and Monuments Record.

For more information, please contact me through The Lympstone Society.

Charlotte Coles

Typical archaeological finds

HISTORICAL LYMPSTONE

Lympstone was known as the "manarellum" or "manarettum", the little manor, in the later Middle Ages, but in spite of its size, it has seen many remarkable events. It is curious, also, how the little manor has been linked with many famous or notorious persons over the centuries.

Lympstone's story starts with pre-history and the Bronze Age. Scatter has been found along the river between Lympstone and Exmouth in an archaeological assessment for the D.o.E. with reference to the Lympstone to Exmouth Sewage Transfer. It was done by Mr. S.D. Turton (ref. DoE/HHR/Exmouth, 1978). In the nineteenth century, George Coventon, a Lympstone fisherman, found a late Bronze Age sword (dated 1,000-800 B.C.) in the river towards Exmouth. These finds indicate Bronze Age settlement nearby. It is also known that in pre-history the landing and the lanes in Lympstone were part of a great trackway, leading from Dorset to Cornwall along the hill tops. This used a ford crossing of the Exe from Lympstone to Starcross on the west side of the Exe estuary. The river must have followed a different course then. A more traceable history goes back to the Romans. Roman coins have been found in Lympstone by the side of the B3180; and a coin of the Emperor Gordianus Pius III (238-244 A.D.) was found in 1879 by the sexton digging a grave in Lympstone churchyard. Both the sword and this coin can be seen in the Royal Albert Museum in Exeter. Another Roman coin, an antoniniarius of Philip I (244-249 A.D.) was dug up more recently in a garden on the Underhill estate. These are signs of Roman presence, though it is unlikely that Lympstone had a villa, as at Budleigh overlooking the Otter, or a port town, as at Topsham. A local man, Mr. George Clapp, however, revealed in an article in the *Express & Echo* of 11th August, 1966, that in about 1860, while digging foundations for the Railway Arch in the middle of the village, workmen uncovered 'an ancient slipway', the timbers of which were made of "bog oak" and had 'been buried for many centuries'. They were believed at the time to have been used by the Romans. Further light has been shed on this in recent times. First, there is oral confirmation in the village of the find, behind the old London Inn by the side of the brook, of a very old slipway. It was understood to be Roman, but was covered over and encased in concrete as part of the flood prevention scheme. This was done by the old Water Board, before the arrival of South West Water. Oral evidence also confirms that (c.1860), foundations of elm had to be put down on what was then the "Marsh", a bog, to support or 'float' the bridge on the marsh, a common practice in the 19th century. The foundations took the form of bundles of elm branches. However, the difference between bundles of elm and "bog oak" must have been visible even in 1960!

Lympstone has been known by many various names, largely on account of the differing phonetic spellings of the scribes. The first known name is given in the Thorn edition of the Domesday Book as Leveston. Another version gives Leustona, also given in 1249 and 1285. A document of 1219 gives Limeneston/Lemineston, and another of 1254 gives Lymeneston. An Inquisition Post Mortem of 1289 refers to Limoneston. A document of Edward I in 1307 gives Loston, and Lanveston; an Exeter scribe's letter to the King of 1310 has "veneston". This was followed elsewhere by Weleston. In 1435 the village was called Limestone; on a map of 1538, Lympston; in Pole's history of 1630, Lemingston but by Risdon, c.1635, Levingston. Then in the 19th century it became Limpston or Lympston etc. The name has come from the Saxon, most probably from "Leofwin's tun" or settlement.

The manor itself, like its name, is of Saxon origin. (The "manor" means an area of land, an estate, usually with a building for the lord of the manor.) Lympstone as we know it today has been formed by the permutations and amalgamations of three small Saxon and Domesday manors, Levenston (Lympstone), Notteswilla (Nutwell) and (almost certainly a Domesday manor) Southedon or Sowden (i.e. south of the down). First one lord of the manor was in the ascendancy, then another. Sowden, in 1330 a separate manor, became part of the manor of Nutwell in 1357, given to Sir John Dynham of Nutwell by charter. Subsequently, it became part of the manor of Lympstone.

About two hundred years after the Roman withdrawal, the Saxons invaded East Devon around 614 A.D., finally gaining control of East Devon in 658 A.D. after a decisive battle at Pinhoe.

There was a Saxon thegn here as lord of the manor of Lympstone before the Conquest (do I need to say 1066). We know this from the Domesday Book of 1086: he was called Saeward. Otherwise, the details of Lympstone in the Domesday Book are disappointingly sparse, even in the much fuller Exeter (Exon) version. Presumably this was because it was in the hands of a reeve and not accounted for by a resident lord. We know that Lympstone was assessed in the Book at one hide and one virgate, which has been translated as about 640 acres by one expert. It had ten villeins (or quite large farmers), six bordars (or smallholders) who both were legally tied to the manor and rendered service for the land they held from the lord, and two slaves (who had no rights or land). If there is no mention of a church or the mill, this does not necessarily mean they did not exist at the time. It is only that documentary evidence first exists later (the Mill is documented in 1228). A county archaeologist has recently said Lower Lympstone has the typical layout of a Saxon manor; it is likely that the half dozen larger houses either side of the railway bridge are on the site of ancient dwellings of the Saxon village.

There is a strong tradition here that there was a church in Saxon times, but if so, being made of wood, nothing of it remains. It is likely that part at any rate of the Saxon village was clustered inland, safe from raiders from the sea. During Saxon times, villagers would have had to keep a look-out for Danish or Viking raiders and would have had to flee with their families and cattle up the old drove roads (Summer Lane - the Parish boundary - and Wotton Lane) to the Commons of Lympstone and Woodbury.

The old Mill

With the Conquest, William the Conqueror imposed a Norman overlord on Lympstone called Richard (who held from the King), son of Count Gilbert (brother of Baldwin the Sheriff), dispossessing the Saxon Saeward. A William Capra then held from him, a sub-tenant and absentee lord, and the manor was held in farm (i.e. for rents to the lord, overseen by a reeve or bailiff, who gave the fines or dues to the lord and he to the next lord up and so to the King).

After reverting to the King because of some misdemeanour of William Capra, the next overlord of Lympstone manor was the holder of the Honour of Braneis (Bradninch), one William de Tracy. William de Tracy was one of the four knights who murdered Archbishop Thomas a' Becket in Canterbury Cathedral in 1170, impelled by some words of Henry II. Henry was so devastated by this that he imposed great penance on all the knights, and William had to give away nearly all his lands and possessions, mainly to churches and monasteries. In 1174, The Honour of Braneis passed with Tracy's daughter, Eva, to William de Courtenay. The lord of the manor and the overlord of the Honour were, however, at that time different. Henry I had given Lympstone to his steward, William Hastings. After some descendants, through marriage Lympstone came into the hands of another Norman family, the de Albemarles (de Alba Mara, d'Aumarle, Damarell, etc.), French knights from Normandy, in 1228. We read: 'Reginald de

The 14th century boss in the Nave of Exeter Cathedral showing Thomas a' Becket, murdered in 1170 by four knights

Albemarle holds Luveneston of Muriel de Bollay, and she of our lord the King in chief by the service of one attendant finding horses together with 1 bow and 5 arrows whenever the King hunts in the forest of Dertemore'. Reginald de Albemarle held Woodbury (formerly a Saxon royal manor) from 1215 (possibly from 1175) and from 1228 he held Lympstone also. Here the long connection of Lympstone with Woodbury began.

In 1251, Reginald divided the manor of Lympstone and created the Rectorial Manor, an unusual step which must have cut his income considerably. However, it was almost *de rigeur* then for lords to give land or money to the Church or the monks so that they would pray frequently for the soul of the donor, for fear of eternal damnation. Reginald may also have been motivated by fear of further lawsuits with his daughter, who took him to court twice for non-payment of gifts he had promised her on marriage. Reginald was a litigious person, and is found at court at Westminster or Wilton or Exeter seven times in the *Feet of Fines*, an account of royal courts then.

The Albemarles were resident Norman lords, the first ones, but it is not known exactly where. Woodbury seems most likely, but so far no Manor House has been identified for certain. The Albemarles used Lympstone church sometimes, for there is a record of an Albemarle baptism there, also because the church at Woodbury had passed from them to Otterton in 1205, thence to the French monastery of St. Michel as the result of a lawsuit. Some time later, it came to the Dean and Chapter of Exeter Cathedral and the Vicars Choral.

Reginald's son William was the next in line. We read from the Hundred of Buddeleg's return that 'William de Albemarle holds the "manarettum" of Luveneston in serjeanty of the King by the service of finding the King TWO arrows and one oaten loaf whenever the King courses on Dertemore'. Note that Lympstone's service to the King had gone down to a serjeanty, and by three arrows to two, from five in Reginald's day. It looks as though Reginald may have sold some land or otherwise devalued the manor. William held Lympstone from 1274 up to 1288 or 1289. William was an entrepreneur. He evidently tried to establish a town at Lympstone, for in 1288 we find "burgesses" or townspeople paying 9s. in dues to William. He managed to gain a grant of a charter and fair for Woodbury from the King in 1288, but established neither a fair at Lympstone nor a town

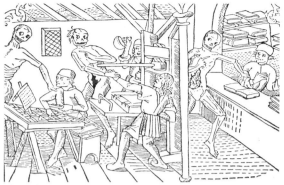

The Black Death haunted peoples' imagination and became
"The Dance of Death"

Effigy of contemporary
de Albemarle cousins in a
West Devon church

The Arms of Geoffrey de Albemarle
as mentioned in the
Great Parliamentary Roll of c. 1312

An illumination showing the building of a church with hoists
and ladder

"whenever The King hunts in the forest of Dertemore"

A battle of The "Wars of the Roses"

(borough charter) at Woodbury nor Lympstone. These ventures would of course have been very lucrative for him, for men attracted to a town would have had to pay for market stalls, water, and burgage plots. He did, however, manage to establish Lympstone as part of the port of Exeter, for in 1310 an important letter from the commonalty of Exeter to the King refers to "veneston" (Lympstone) as a member of the port. Maryanne Kowaleski in her article on 14th century ports places Lympstone on the map as a well-known port on the Exe, presumably with seamen and ships' masters and a fishing trade as well.

The next man in was another Galfride or Geoffrey de Albemarle who held both Lympstone and Woodbury again, from 1303-1320. One incident stands out during his time: we note in Edward Ist's State Papers that 'Ten tuns of wine were cast ashore on the land of Geoffrey Daumare of Woodbury and Lanveston from a ship wrecked between Dartmue and Exemue'. Now a tun or cask held 240 gallons of wine! What treasure to land on a small manor, 2,400 gallons of wine, and what celebrations there must have been!

Geoffrey was followed by another William, who was made a knight in 1326. Sir William de Albemarle may have been the sponsor of the beginning of the rebuilding of Lympstone church, since it was in his time in 1329 that the then Rector, Richard de Doune, requested Bishop de Grandisson to postpone 'consecrating the church because it was only new in parts (in quandum sui parte nova est constructa)'. Sir William died in 1346, the time of the coming of the Plague. He was followed by yet another Sir William, who was referred to as Sir William Damarell. His heir, another William, died young in 1363 (from the Black Death?). When he, the last Albemarle, died, his sisters inherited his estates. It was the eldest sister who had married William Bonville of Shute, that inherited Lympstone, taking the dues from the manor and the Manor Court with her. Here it seems the connection between Lympstone and Woodbury ceased. She was, however, very probably the benefactress of Lympstone church who gave it its tower, as she did for Woodbury church.

She and her husband were spared the horrors of the Wars of the Roses, dying in 1407 and 1408 but their descendants were involved. In these Wars, in 1455, the William Bonville of the day and the Earl of Devon fought a battle on Lympstone shore. Later, in further battles, the Bonville father, son and grandson perished, wiping out the line. The one-year old Cecily Bonville was left the richest heiress in England. It is not surprising that when she was thirteen in 1474, she was married off to King Edward IV's stepson, Thomas Grey, then Marquis of Dorset. In this way it came about that Cecily's great-greatgranddaughter was the famous Lady Jane Grey who was beheaded, with her father, in 1554. Lympstone was part of the marriage settlement made to Frances Brandon, mother of Lady Jane Grey, and for this reason was not forfeit to the Crown when Lady Jane Grey was beheaded. Frances Brandon, however, eventually disposed of the manor.

The next lord of the manor came into Lympstone in 1557 when Lympstone, and Woodbury, were sold to John Prideaux of Nutwell Manor, Sergeant-at-Law. He was the first of a number of rich London lawyers to come to Nutwell. The Prideaux family owned estates in Cornwall and Dorset, two of which were acquired when Henry VIII abolished the monasteries. John Prideaux bought the Nutwell estates, which included Lympstone, from Lord Zouch, who had acquired them from his wife Joan, second daughter of the Lord John Dynham who was the last of the line to live at Nutwell Court. John Prideaux was succeeded by his son Thomas, his grandson Thomas, and his great-grandson Thomas.

Elizabethan times - a portrait of the young Ralegh

In Elizabethan times (1558-1603) under the first John Prideaux, there lived in the village, it is believed, a Ralph Lane, soldier and equerry of the Queen, who went on Ralegh's second expedition to the New World in 1585, and founded a colony on Roanoke Island, which underwent great hardship and deprivation, and was attacked by the natives. Rescued by Drake with the survivors, Ralph Lane came back to be present at the Armada. (A direct descendant, Samuel Lane, a fisherman, went to London from Lympstone in 1821 and became a publican and music-hall proprietor. Lupino Lane was descended from him!) The above suggests a strong connection between the Ralegh brothers and Lympstone, and indeed it has been suggested that the half-brothers of Sir Walter may have built and sailed their privateers (from which the family gained great wealth) from Lympstone.

Lympstone was then apparently well-known for its ships' carpenters, for several were engaged by Exeter city to help build a ship, the "Gyfte", for Queen Elizabeth which saw action at the Armada.

A painting of the type of ship built in Lympstone in medieval times

There is even an earlier reference to shipbuilding at Lympstone in an old account roll of the Manor for Michaelmas (September) 1430-Michaelmas 1431. "Scaffoe" were the wooden supports round which a ship would be built 'at the seaside' at Lympstone for which use of the shore, the Lord would charge. Indeed, Lympstone has been important in shipbuilding, maritime ventures and trade, in the late 16th, 17th and particularly the 18th centuries. Yet it is still so often referred to as 'the little old-world fishing village' (Delderfield) or 'Lympstone has been both fishing village and agricultural settlement' (E.A.G. Clark), which while being undoubtedly true so far, do Lympstone less than justice. These statements totally ignore Lympstone's large part in the maritime economy of the River Exe and its connection with the sea which was altogether broader and more important than the inshore fishing. Fishing there certainly has been, as a fall-back position, early on and after 1830 particularly, but only when circumstances brought entrepreneurs, merchants, ship-owners and shipbuilders to a halt.

For instance, even as early as 1573 (in Elizabeth's reign) there is an account of the "John of Lympstone" foundering at the mouth of the Exe on return from Newfoundland. The Newfoundland trade which was the mainstay of Lympstone for two and a half centuries was even then evolving. It involved trade with salt and Exeter cloths to Newfoundland; with salted cod from Newfoundland to the Catholic

Breast hook or floor knee, and floor timber found during excavations for the sewage works in Lympstone in May, 1985

countries of the Mediterranean, Portugal, Spain, France and Italy, and return journeys laden with wines, fruit, silk, salt and other goods. This staple trade continued in spite of the advent of wars on the Continent, and piracy in English waters, and led to huge fortunes being made and prosperous merchants who built large houses in Lympstone.

Piracy in English waters was rife off the coast of Devon in the 16th and 17th centuries. Foreign pirates, generically called "Turks", were very active. Throughout the earlier and the Stuart period, West Country shipping suffered severe losses through Turkish pirates from Algiers and the dreaded rovers of Sallee. At one period in 1638, no less than 15 Turkish pirate vessels were cruising off the South Coast of Devon, and were able to anchor with impunity in Torbay and under the lee of Start Point. Sailors faced capture, being sold in the slave markets along the Barbary coast, becoming galley-slaves and in many cases, being tortured most horribly, including having their tongues cut out. Evidence of these fates is revealed in some petitions in the Exeter Quarter Sessions papers, from Lympstone Masters and sailors unable to pay their ransoms, or petitions from their friends and relations. One petition 'showeth that William Blight of our pish (parish) of Limpston in ye County of Devon went away in a shippe belonging to the port of Exon. And about a yeare and a half Since was taken by three Salley men of Warre by whom he is detained in moste miserable Captivity to this day'. The petitioner was one Elizabeth Reede of Limpston in 1673. The "Ransome" amounted to fifty pounds 'which is a sum Altogether disproportionate to his Ability to procure, For he being a poore man, and of about Fifty six years of Age ...' , which caused Elizabeth to ask for help 'from Christians, the Honble. Gentry and the Reverend Clergy', or for help 'out of the late Publique Charity to that intent'. Another petition was from a Robert Moxey of Lympston to the county justices, who helped because he was a poor man and not able to pay the £17.10s. There are many such petitions - in collections in Topsham, in Honiton Churchwardens' Accounts of 1618, by the High Sheriff of Exeter in 1631-43, by the Churchwardens' Accounts for the parish of Littleham in 1679, and so on. Indeed the list is huge, not only in Devon but in England as a whole.

It was not only the "Turks", however, who practised piracy. There were English pirates, too, who had long had the backing of the State in providing "privateers". They were given "Letters of Marque" to provide justification for their actions. They preyed on enemy shipping and at times protected English shipping from the "Turks" or the French.

Any prize money was shared out with the crew, but the largest share of course went to the captain. John Nutt of Lympstone is recorded in State papers of 1623 as a pirate: he enjoyed the patronage of one Secretary of State as a privateer, whilst he was arrested as a pirate on the orders of another! John Nutt's brother and family were involved. We have already seen that in the late 16th century, Sir Walter Ralegh's half-brothers were privateers.

In the Civil War, under the Parliamentarian Prideaux at Nutwell, Lympstone was largely Parliamentarian. It is thought cannon were fired from the Cliff Field, trying to prevent supplies and reinforcements getting through to the then Royalist Exeter. It is also thought that both sides used the church tower for sightings by which to fire their cannon. Cannon balls have been found in various gardens in the village, one at Redcliffe, another very near the Green by the river. (Cliff Field, above the Boat Shelter, is now cared for by the National Trust and has a wide view over the estuary to the Haldon Hills and up the river to Exeter. It can be approached by a footpath behind the Swan Inn.)

During and after the Civil War, it was not only the choice between the King and Cromwell that caused difficulties, however. It was a difficult time for the clergy, too. After Dionysius Prideaux (presented by his father, Sir Thomas Prideaux in 1630), an Edmund Rowe became Rector in 1640. He had to take a stand about the growing number of Dissenters (Presbyterians and Unitarians) in his parish. At first they were only allowed to worship in specially licensed houses, (e.g. Filmores), then they were persecuted under the Restoration's Act of Uniformity of 1662. Edmund Rowe signed this Declaration in favour of Church and State in August, 1662. After the Act of Toleration was passed in 1689, however, the Dissenters built a chapel at Gulliford on the boundaries of Woodbury and Lympstone which attracted a great number of people. This alternative worship must have caused the Revd Rowe some dismay. However, he remained quiet and retained his benefice until his death, which was more than the Vicar of Woodbury. He had to resign because of the 'agitations of religious opinion' and because he did not sign the Declaration. In fact, he came to the Gulliford Dissenters' Chapel in 1689 to be the minister there.

In 1675, the manor of Lympstone was sold eventually by Sir John Prideaux' great-grandson to Sir Thomas Putt of Coombe (after whom the apple "Tom Putt" is named). His son, another Sir Thomas, was well in advance of his times, for when most villagers were still part of a semi-feudal estate, he gave instructions that on his death his tenants might buy the freeholds of their properties with full manorial rights - an almost unheard of step! Sir Thomas was deeply in debt when he died in 1721, so he ordered the sale of most of Lympstone manor, excluding the waste (lands) and a few rights. Several of the houses built on land bought in 1722 still bear the name of independent villagers - Basses, Manston's, the former Smith's, Teed's and others. (Indeed then and later, many of the houses in the village have retained the name of former owners - Hare's, for instance, Mitchell's, Stafford House, White's Cottages, Metherell's and Sheppard's.)

1721 was when the manor began to break up, for so many Lympstone people bought their freeholds, also common rights for grazing, hunting, shooting, fishing and for underwood and sand (this for 2d. paid at Michaelmas each year!). There was not much of the manor left, though the Putts retained this for many years. There then came one more connection with the famous, for the Putts first leased the manor of Lympstone to Sir Francis Drake of Buckland Abbey, the third baronet, then sold the lordship of Lympstone in 1802 to Lord Heathfield of Nutwell, who had married a Drake. Thus began the long connection of Lympstone and the Drakes.

In 1711, Gertrude (Drake) Pollexfen's younger Drake sister, Frances, came to live in Sowden hamlet. '... Frances and Henry Drake left Netherton, in Buckland Monachorum, and settled at Souton House, in the parish of Lympstone. Sir Francis's son-in-law, Henry Drake ... was buried at Lympstone on 4th May, 1718': so says Lady Elliott Drake in her book *The Family and Heirs of Sir Francis Drake*. Frances and Henry Drake's memorial slabs are still in the nave of the Church at Lympstone, (one being invisible under the new altar platform) after being initially placed with the family tombs in the north aisle. *(See Drake family tree page 23)*

The eighteenth century was the great age of affluence in the village. The mariners of Lympstone, together with those of Topsham and the merchants of Exeter, built and furbished ships and traded to Europe, particularly Holland, and to America and Newfoundland. There was also the coastal and the short sea trade. Names such as the Withalls, the Staffords, the Brices and the Basses, all shipbuilders, are prominent in Lympstone. The Basses, important shipwrights, owned a huge property, from the end of Quay Lane to the limekiln now by the Boat Shelter and on back into the hinterland up the Brook at least as far as Strawberry Hill, with its many orchards. They built Newfoundland merchantmen, coastal traders, and later, ships for the Navy. The Withalls, like the Staffords, sailed their own ships and even had members of their own family in Newfoundland and Spain to act as their agents. In 1743, one of the Withall ships, the "Elizabeth", was valued at £350 and her cargo at £858, which represented enormous wealth. Mrs. Elizabeth Scott states that when Henry Withall died on the Newfoundland voyage, he had with him four brothers. It looks very much as though ship-owning and investment in the Newfoundland trade was a family affair. Worthington Brice, of whom more anon, at one time shared the Bass shipyard from the Green to where the Methodist Chapel now stands. He built Newfoundland merchantmen, coastal traders and, later on, privateers and Greenland whalers.

Boatbuilding was very big business in Lympstone from the 17th century right through the 18th and continued into the 19th century. Many of the ships, it is thought, were on mud berths. Apart from trade, travelling by sea was still the most convenient way to reach Exeter, London and of course France and Holland. The families connected with shipbuilding and trade became extremely prosperous; they built themselves houses here. There were a number of excellent shipwrights in the village who, when not shipbuilding, built the beautiful staircases, fireplaces, panels and floors in many of the houses. There was "gentrification" of older farmhouses, which were modernized and refronted. Many forms of building materials can be seen now in the village from cob-and-thatch to Georgian brick. Limestone was processed at the two large limekilns near the boat shelter and was also used - and Dutch bricks, smaller in size than the local ones, were brought back as ballast from the Low Countries, Holland, and used here. They can often be seen in the chimney stacks.

The Manor House and Greenhill, both elegant houses built in the 18th century, were mostly let to visitors coming south for health and social reasons. All these residences must have given a lot of employment at every level in the village, both inside and out. There were at one time thirty or forty shops and in addition dress-makers, laundresses, shoe-makers, saddlers, wheelwrights and lace-makers. There was even a School for Young Ladies at Brook Cottage; 'special attention to Morals, Health and Manners, Ladies under ten, £22 per annum, Ladies over ten, £26 per annum'.

However, the balance of trade on the Exe was altering. In the second half of the 18th century, the cloth and serge trade had been declining overall, and while trade from Topsham to Holland continued, ports such as Bristol and London and those further north captured the last remaining cloth trade which was now in the north. Then came the wars - the Dutch, the French, the American War of Independence, the Revolutionary and Napoleonic wars. All created difficulties for commerce, with closure of European markets and decline and great difficulties for the Newfoundland trade. There was also the press gang for the Navy in Britain, making for depletion of the labour force.

It was in this way that Lympstone became involved during the second half of the 18th century with whale fishing in the Arctic. This, for Lympstone, was to be an alternative trade to the Newfoundland fishing (which still continued) and a second string to shipbuilding. The Exeter Whale Fishing Company was formed by Matthew Lee of Ebford in 1754 and the Lympstone shipbuilder, Worthington Brice, now of Parsonage Stile House, was a very active member and share-holder. Worthington Brice, originally of Exton, then of Lympstone, had purchased land from the then impoverished Sir Francis Henry Drake, and built wharves and a yard for shipbuilding by Parsonage Stile bay.

The Exeter Whale Fishing Company seemingly came about firstly because there assembled at Gulliford Dissenters' Chapel many local and Exeter entrepreneurs and merchants, and ideas passed quickly round the congregation or outside after the service. The merchants came to hear that the British Government, in order to try to outdo the Dutch, were giving a subsidy to all British whaling ships on the collection of valuable whale oil. The whaling ports were mainly in the north-east, far away, in places like Grimsby and Hull. However, the possibilities of this trade appealed to Matthew Lee and others, and so the Exeter company was inaugurated - the only such enterprise in all the south-west.

Greenland Fishery: English Whalers in the ice. Artist: Charles Brooking, 18th Century painter 1723-1759

Parsonage Stile House from an old oil painting

The ship Worthington Brice bought for the company in 1754 was of 346 tons, and cost £2,150. She was brought back to Brice's Yard at Parsonage Stile to be fitted out and victualled. The ship's first voyage to Greenland commenced on 18th April, 1755 and she returned on 9th August, four months later.

These voyages were very dangerous, not only because of Arctic weather but because of the danger of being trapped and crushed in the ice. This fate in fact happened to the Exeter Company's ship "The Worthy Shepherd" in 1759. Next, there was the danger of the boat being smashed to pieces by the whale's massive tail. Nevertheless, the "Exeter" continued on the annual voyage until 1780 and the "Lympstone" until 1787.

The brief summer months were the only time the boats could remain in the Arctic, so the boats had to bring the blubber home for boiling into oil. The smell of the oil and of the 'horrible mass of putridity landed from the tanks of the Greenland whalers' could not have been very pleasant! The layers of blubber and the valuable head oil were first removed from the carcasses by sailors using long-handled flensing knives; the blubber was then returned to the Exe, some of it to be boiled on Dawlish Warren. Worthington Brice, however, had his tryworks for boiling the blubber in his yard at Parsonage Stile, whence the noxious smell reached the whole village when the wind was right! (*See Map and key overleaf.*)

An old oil painting of Parsonage Stile Bay, long before the railway, showing the whale-oil barrels being ferried in and out from Worthington Brice's Yard at Parsonage Stile

Apart from the very valuable whale oil, whale bone was prized for making numerous objects - sieves and riddles, nets for folding sheep, stays for weavers, grating for granary, barn and warehouse windows, ornamental blinds, umbrella ribs, hoops for crinolines and stay bones, etc. The enormous whale vertebrae were frequently used by butchers for chopping blocks. When old cottages were pulled down in 1912 to make room for the new Lord Roberts' Institute, the jawbone of a whale was found built into the doorway of one of them. It was then thrown out onto the beach where it remained for some years. The summerhouse of Matthew Lee at Ebford apparently also had a whale's jawbone surrounding its door. Whale jaws could be

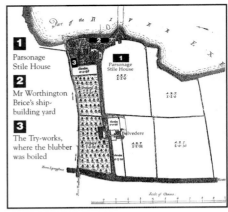

1 Parsonage Stile House

2 Mr Worthington Brice's ship-building yard

3 The Try-works, where the blubber was boiled

Map showing the location of Parsonage Stile House

seen some years ago built into the wall at Sowden End, but are now covered over by a repair.

Worthington Brice lived in the lovely old thatched house at Parsonage Stile, burned down in 1932 *(see picture p.17)*. This had been an inn before his time, alleged to be a haunt of smugglers. Worthington Brice did not live to see the end of the Exeter Whale Fishing Company, which was wound up when the subsidy on whale oil was discontinued by the Government in 1787. He died in 1781, in his eightieth year and is buried in the Unitarian Burial Ground at Gulliford, where his gravestone can be seen. *(See chapter on Gulliford, page 28)*

There was another, less honourable trade for Lympstonians in the 18th century, which was widespread in the south-west and indeed all along the coast of England. This was smuggling, which had gone on for centuries, and was considered acceptable by many sections of the community, from squires, parsons and innkeepers looking for spirits and tobacco at untaxed cost, to mariners, runners, look-outs and storage men looking for a good return. Nevertheless, it was estimated in 1783 that smuggling was depriving the Government of at least two million pounds in revenue a year, a colossal sum. 'A halcyon time', says M. Oppenheim, and 'Much of Devon's seamanship was exercised in the practice of smuggling which turned out first-class seamen'. The 1733 Parliamentary Committee's 'figures of seizures are incomplete, but most of those noted took place in Exeter and at places in or near the Exe estuary'. Many of the Lympstone cottages near the river have nooks and crannies where smuggled goods were hidden. A Lympstonian, Mr. Coventon, remembered as a child seeing goods hidden in the chimney of the present Limekilns. Some cottages have spaces in adjoining roofs where contraband was said to be passed from house to house. One record is that tobacco and tubs were taken by smugglers from Teignmouth, passing over Lower Haldon to Powderham, 'where Boats have been in readiness to tow the Goods ... to Lympstone on the River Exe at any time after dusk ... Lympstone is as free and open for Contrabandists as any Smuggler could wish ... consequently a notorious haunt of Smugglers ...' So says H.J. Trump, author of *Westcountry Harbour*, a book on Teignmouth. Another account is that there were smugglers' runs at Parsonage Stile and at Sowden End; smugglers lured the Preventive

Officers to that run where boats were not coming in by means of brandy or tobacco! Certainly at one time Lympstone appeared so suspect that four Preventive Officers lived opposite the Globe Inn. Sowden Farm had large hiding-places in the barns and Sowden House, on the run to the Common, has several in the house. There is said to have been a secret tunnel leading to the Beach from the House and two people in living memory are said to have been down it, both meeting a fall of earth. So far nothing has been found. Apparently Rogues Roost, then up Wotton Lane, was used as a stage in the journey of goods over the Common, also Bee Cottage up towards Lympstone Common. Goods were put in a cart, covered with mangels and taken off to markets at Woodbury, East Budleigh and elsewhere.

Later in the 18th century, because of very high taxation on spirits, wine and tobacco, and because of the shortages caused by the wars, smuggling was at its height. As Mrs. Elizabeth Scott has said, it was when Mr. Gidoin was Rector (1782 onwards). This was according to some local family accounts, which also stated that all along the coast people were fearful of a French invasion. They were making preparations to flee inland when Bonaparte invaded. An old lady then living at Sowden House used to tell how 'they had money sewn up inside their stays and horses ready in the stables so that they might set off for Dartmoor when the warning beacons were lit!'

Fear of Napoleon not only changed people's plans, it altered the roads too. The roads improved both south and north of Lympstone for the military. Lord Heathfield at Nutwell completed a wall round the estate, it is said by French prisoner labour, and also completed the "New Road" round Nutwell originally planned by Sir Francis Henry Drake. This was in order that people did not walk through Nutwell as before from Exmouth along the river to Exeter, but walked outside the wall.

Sir Digby Forest, a retired Admiral, Secretary to three Commanders-in-Chief, who had been present at both the battles of Copenhagen and Trafalgar, may also have been instrumental in changing the pattern of the roads in Lympstone. Knighted by the Prince Regent, he lived at Bridgethorpe in the village on retirement. His stables (now Exeleigh) were above his house on what was then the main road from Exmouth, across the Marsh, up the hill past the stables - and on to Nutwell and Exeter. Sir Digby was famous for driving his carriage and four downhill at speed, scattering anyone in his way and turning sharply into the village street, a great feat which scared the villagers. The road was really only the width for a packhorse. (Shortly after, Sir Digby moved to the Beacon in Exmouth, the first house owner there, before the Ladies Byron and Nelson.) Whether this influenced Sir George Burgmann, a Dutch merchant who lived at what he called "The Cottage" from 1822 (now Thornbury) to give some of his land to build a new road is not known, but he did and the new King's Highway was originally called "Lady Burgmann's Hill". Captain Adney at Highcliffe House also got the road past his house altered. Pump Lane was abandoned, and the present Sowden Lane (called Cox's Hill by the older generation) created.

So things were changing in the early 19th century. Sadly, shipbuilding, which was the mainstay of Lympstone for centuries and particularly the eighteenth, was ending with the post-war slump, and the introduction of much larger steam ships, made of iron. Many of the skilled men took their families to Plymouth and the Dockyard and to Wales where they could find jobs. The possibility of the railway, discussed for years and eventually arriving in 1861, also threatened the shipbuilders, the line finally cutting them off from the water.

In 1833 came the Great Fire of Lympstone, when 58 cottages were burned down in Quay Lane and a small area of the Strand and well over 240 people were made homeless. This started as a result of a pan of mackerel catching alight in a fisherman's cottage. The fire spread through most of the cottages by the river and up to the Green, their thatched roofs rapidly catching fire. The Poor House also burned down. Such a disaster affected not only the homeless, but also the layout of the village. When they were re-built, the new houses in the Strand and Quay Lane were of stone, brick and slate, no longer mainly cob and thatch, and many no longer looked out onto the water. Then after long preparations and purchase of land, came the railway, opening in 1861. Mrs. Rosemary Burton has said that it cut through people's gardens and orchards, brought argument and contention and later, soot blowing everywhere. She continued that anybody who was anybody removed from near the railway and, as has been pointed out, the great disaster occurred of shipbuilding coming to an end, being cut off from the water. Fishing remained as a fall-back position and continued, however, and no doubt profited by better communications. Indeed in White's *Devon Gazeteer and Directory* of 1850 Lympstone is said to be '... a pretty townlet ... with a great trade in shippes ... a fishing station having about 60 small fishing boats and large beds of oysters in the estuary'.

Around the beginning of the 19th century, there still took place an event which must have been happening since medieval times. The Rector, the Revd Charles Gordon Browne, writing in 1909 said: 'There are still old people in the Parish who remember the vanished glories of the Lympstone Fair. This used to be held on the Wednesday after St. Swithun's Day, pointing to some former connection between this Parish and Woodbury'. He went on to say that after the Parish Clerk had proclaimed the Fair from the church porch, people came in from all the countryside and the pleasure booths extended from the bottom of the Rectory Hill (now Burgmann's) to Highcliffe. Unfortunately he continues by saying that the chief glory of the Fair was the Bullring. Bullbaiting was then a top sport. 'The bull used to be brought in by what is still called the 'New' Road ... past the Rectory. The young and elder folks used to go out to meet him and escort him to the shed where he spent the night. Next day, numbers of shoemakers from Crediton, most of whom kept bulldogs, brought their animals over and a grand bull bait took place ...'

What is important here is that the Revd Gordon Browne's assumption that this Lympstone Fair was connected with Woodbury's St. Swithun's Fair in older times is correct, for there was a joint holding of the manors at the time of the Albemarles. The Fair implies a large and thriving Lympstone in medieval times, as only villages of a certain size and importance were given the right to hold them.

In the early and mid-19th century, the population was gradually rising until 1861, according to the Census figures studied by Dr. Sellman. He says there was large-scale migration from the parish, approximately 320 people in the first half of the century, and 370 in the second half, about 40% of the population. This must show the effects of the end of shipbuilding and also of the attraction of America, Canada and Australia. However, there was a certain amount of building going on too, as can be seen by the number of Victorian houses and cottages in the village. Apart from smaller ones, five large houses were constructed: Harefield, first mentioned in 1826, owned from 1846 by the Peters family; Strawberry Hill, later known as The Grange, first mentioned in the 1841 Census; Lympstone House, first built on the opposite side of the road with its garden in its present position, and first mentioned in the 1861 Census; and Tedstone House, first mentioned in the 1861 Census. They were all large, with big gardens which no doubt gave work to local people. For the poor and the fishermen, Mrs. William Henry Peters had the cottages by the harbour built, and to commemorate her, William Henry Peters built the Peters' Tower, a landmark for all who sailed. It is now in the hands of the Landmark Trust as a holiday let. The late Admiral Sir Arthur Peters, Mrs. Peter's grand-son, lived at Harefield until it was taken over by a preparatory school after World War II.

Harefield House

In the mid-19th century, the Rector and the Parochial Church Council at the Easter Vestry of 1862 decided that the church would have to be re-built, such was its dilapidation. Mr. Edward Ashworth, the architect, was instructed to draw up plans and the old church was last used on 1st February, 1863, and demolition began. Fortunately, we have an account of the medieval church which was being brought down, from the Revd Fulford who came to witness it from Woodbury (probably on his tricycle, his favourite method of transport!). He talks of the wonderful colour of the interior, with roof and mural decoration, also coloured texts painted on the walls. Indeed, the church must 'once have been all glorious within'. (For a full description, see *A Short History and Guide to Lympstone Parish Church* by Rosemary Smith.) The church was re-built and consecrated in July 1864, by the Bishop of Jamaica, acting for the old, infirm Bishop of Exeter. It is very much as we see it today, with the exception of two enlargements to the chancel of 1831 and 1928.

Another important event of the late 19th century was the inauguration of the Parish Council in December, 1894. The first Chairman was Mr. W.S. Quick, and the first meeting took place in the Boys' School room. The eleven Councillors (as today) elected were: The Revd Gordon Browne, Mr. Quick, Mr. W.S. Jackson, Mr. Williams, Mr. Arscott, Mr. Hayman, Mr. Reed, Mr. Grant, Mr. Venus, Mr. Mortimer, and Mr. Pidsley.

The Revd Charles Gordon Browne

The Clerk to the Parish Council was then Mr. R. Venman, who had previously been the Deputy Overseer to the Parish, at a salary of £25 per annum. The names of all Chairmen and Clerks can now be seen on the Roll of Honour Board in the Village Hall Function Room. It is to be noted that Miss Dorothy Jackson, who took over as Parish Clerk after her father, was in the post from 1926-1973 or 1974.

Around the years 1894-96, street lighting was introduced to Lympstone. Fourteen oil lamps had to be lit one hour after sunset and to be extinguished at 11p.m. After a number of years, these oil lamps were changed to gas lamps, then to electricity (probably when electricity came to the village in the 1930s).

One of the last important events in 19th century Lympstone was the petition by Lympstone fishermen to the Parish Council in 1895, asking for assistance in building a shelter for their boats. At a meeting in the Girls' School room in March, 1895, it was agreed that as the cost could not go on the rates, everyone in the Parish should be asked for voluntary contributions. The 44 fishermen in the village agreed to contribute also, paying sums of two shillings upwards, and gave their labour too. There is a list of contributors from the village, including Lady Drake, the Rector and William Peters, also Viscountess Chetwynd and Charles Louch, but also from many villagers. Work

Fishermen who built the old Boat Shelter in 1895

continued until the Shelter was finished in 1897.

This Fishermen's Shelter was unfortunately almost totally destroyed by a storm in 1912. The fishermen continued some years without a shelter and some boats were damaged. However, by February, 1935, a committee had been formed to carry out work on a new shelter, and the laying of the foundation stones had taken place 'in the presence of a large gathering of boatmen and villagers, presided over by Captain C.P. Shrubb...' Mr. D.W. Salter was the honorary architect, and Mr. J. Wannell the masonry instructor. Work on the masonry was carried out voluntarily, and Mr. Veale, the honorary Secretary to the Boat Shelter committee, presented Sir Garbutt Knott, Major J. Barton Aiken and Mr. Norman A.H. Jenkin with ivory-handled trowels with which to lay the foundation stones. Sir Garbutt Knott laid the first stone and placed upon it a silver coin of the realm: he was followed by Major Aiken and Mr. Norman Jenkin. Mr. C.F. Venus then thanked the gentlemen on behalf of the fishermen and said they greatly appreciated the help they had received. Mr. G. A. Norton then proposed a vote of thanks to Captain Shrubb, who replied saying he had received apologies from the Earl of Devon and Mr. Cedric Drewe, M.P., for their absence. The ceremony ended with a verse of the National Anthem.

The Cliff and Old Boat Shelter, Lympstone

Afterwards, there were long months of voluntary work on the walls, and Sir Garbutt Knott is said to have encouraged the building work by taking the volunteers to the local pub in the late morning! The new Boat Shelter was dedicated in 1936, with bunting flying and crowds gathered, and it is still important to the sailors and villagers of Lympstone. There are sadly no working fishermen left, but the Shelter is now enjoyed by the members of the Sailing Club and sailors of Lympstone.

What was left of Lympstone Manor seems to have gone to Mr. Northcott at Nutwell, then his daughter, Mrs. Clarke. This was when Lady Seaton's (Elizabeth Fuller Elliott Drake's) heir, Mr. Meyrick, sold out at Nutwell in 1938. Mrs. Clarke was the last known owner of Lympstone manor and the foreshore. However, in 2005, the latter is now in the hands of the Lympstone Fishery and Harbour Association. It was bought from Mrs. Clarke's estate and the Association's constitution protects it as a village amenity. Lympstone is one of the three owners of the Exe foreshore - the others are the Crown and the Earl of Devon! The Rectorial Manor continued until about the mid-1930s, but almost the last mention of it was when the Revd Gordon Browne said he was prepared to charge the Council One Penny per year to keep the manor rights in 1895. He considered the land for the Shelter to be in the Rectory Manor.

The opening of the new Boat Shelter, 1936

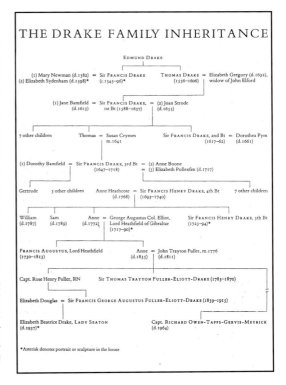

THE DRAKE FAMILY INHERITANCE

EDMUND DRAKE

(1) Mary Newman (d.1582) = Sir FRANCIS DRAKE   THOMAS DRAKE = Elizabeth Gregory (d.1632), widow of John Elford
(2) Elizabeth Sydenham (d.1598)*   (c.1545-96)*   (1556-1606)

(1) Jane Bamfield = Sir FRANCIS DRAKE, = (2) Joan Strode
   (d.1613)   1st Bt (1588-1637)   (d.1655)

7 other children   Thomas = Susan Crymes   Sir FRANCIS DRAKE, 2nd Bt = Dorothea Pym
   m.1641   (1617-62)   (d.1661)

(1) Dorothy Bamfield = Sir FRANCIS DRAKE, 3rd Bt = (2) Anne Boone
   (1647-1718) = (3) Elizabeth Pollexfen (d.1717)

Gertrude   3 other children   Anne Heathcote = Sir FRANCIS HENRY DRAKE, 4th Bt   7 other children
   (d.1768)   (1693-1740)

William   Sam   Anne = George Augustus Col. Elliot,   Sir FRANCIS HENRY DRAKE, 5th Bt
(d.1787)   (d.1789)   (d.1772)   Lord Heathfield of Gibraltar   (1723-94)*
   (1717-90)*

FRANCIS AUGUSTUS, Lord Heathfield   Anne = John Trayton Fuller, m.1776
(1730-1813)   (d.1835)   (d.1811)

Capt. Rose Henry Fuller, RN   Sir THOMAS TRAYTON FULLER-ELIOTT-DRAKE (1785-1870)

Elizabeth Douglas = Sir FRANCIS GEORGE AUGUSTUS FULLER-ELIOTT-DRAKE (1839-1915)

Elizabeth Beatrice Drake, LADY SEATON   Capt. RICHARD OWEN-TAPPS-GERVIS-MEYRICK
(d.1937)*   (d.1964)

*Asterisk denotes portrait or sculpture in the house

Rosemary Smith, M.A., 2005

(This section has been compiled from original research by Rosemary Smith. She has also consulted the work of Rosemary Burton and Ursula Perry. She wishes particularly to acknowledge the work of the Revd Charles Gordon Browne, Miss Howard, Mrs. Elizabeth Scott's *Lympstone: a Village Story* and Mrs. Mary Insull's *Lympstone Heritage*, also the work of Dr. Sellman. She has also consulted works such as *The Victoria County History of Devon, Vol. 1*, [the only volume written]; M. Oppenheim, *The Maritime History of Devon*; *The New Maritime History of Devon, Volumes I and II*, various editors; M. Kowaleski, *The Local Customs Accounts of the Port of Exeter*, etc. etc.)

MILITARY HISTORY

Although Lympstone's military history extends back over the centuries few details survive, and to date, one of the earliest records specifically naming Lympstonians is the Militia Muster Roll of 1597. This detailed 20 men by name as archers, harquebusiers, pikemen and billmen.

During the Civil War the Prideaux of Nutwell for Parliament, and the Courtenays of Powderham for the King, had been glaring at each other across the estuary. In 1645, a Parliamentarian battery was established in Cliff Field to bombard Powerham Castle and on 4th December of that year the Nutwell garrison, under a Captain Farmer, sallied forth across the estuary to attack the castle. However, unknown to the attackers, the castle had been reinforced by Royalist troops from Exeter a few hours earlier, causing the attack to fail and the would-be attackers to be besieged in Kenton Church.

Lympstone being an inland port many of its young men, not unnaturally, became seafarers; men like Edward Nosworthy, born 1766, fought in Nelson's fleet at the Battle of the Nile as a Gunner's Mate and was killed at the Battle of Trafalgar. It seems that some time previously, when Nelson was a Captain on half pay, he and his wife stayed at Bronte House, opposite Ye Old Saddlers' Inn. In 1797 French prisoners of war built the long Nutwell wall under the directions of a Woodbury builder. The Parish records note in the same year the Constable, Ambrose Hearn, acquiring lead for musket balls for the militiamen and in 1798 submitting a list of men, carts and carthorses to the High Constable, apparently in accordance with plans to 'drive the country' in case of a French landing. In 1803 the 68 men of The Lympstone Light Infantry, along with other Volunteers in the County, received a unanimous vote of thanks from the House of Commons.

Traces are still discernible of the three firing points of a three hundred yard musketry range firing into Target Cove, one of the coves beneath Cliff Field: the range must have

Lympstone Home Guard, 1944
Back left to right: Lloyd England, George Morrish, Vick Norton, Tom (Snips) Stamp
Front left to right: Alf Langmead, Jack Haydon, Captain Young, Dick Adams, Fred Blight, Richard Vanstone

pre-dated 1889, the first date it appeared on the OS map but it is quite possible that at one time it had been where the archers practised. Also appearing for the first time on the OS maps of 1889 was the Drill Hall alongside Cliff Field, which was the base for several types of volunteer Artillerymen: old age eventually overtook its fabric and it was demolished in 1947. About the only trace in recent years was the concrete plinth on the other side of the hedge from the Scout Hut in Cliff Field; the plinth bore marks of bearing rings for two Coast Defence drill purpose guns.

The Great War broke out in 1914 and in October 1915 the Lord Lieutenant called for the names of those in uniform to be published in a Roll of Honour. This recorded the name, initials, rank and unit of 123 Lympstonians, including the names of two Red Cross nurses and one munitions worker. The 1911 Census Return had recorded a total population of 999 men, women and children and out of the 446 adult males noted, 120 or 26.9% were named in the Roll of Honour as serving in HM Forces with many more volunteering after 1915. The Village War Memorial names 27 making the ultimate sacrifice and the outline of their service history is recorded in the Book of Remembrance which rests in the Parish Church.

In WW2 Lympstone and Exton provided a Home Guard Platoon in which some 164 men and 6 women telephonists served at one time or another. The names of four Lympstonians are recorded on the Village War Memorial as having paid the ultimate sacrifice in WW2, two in the first two weeks of hostilities.

In 1940, in the face of an imminent German invasion, all local civil responsibilities were made the concern of local Invasion committees. Unlike the general strategy of the Napoleonic era which had called for the local populace to 'fly the country', in 1940 there was to be a general stand-fast to free the roads for the military. Local Invasion Committees were each charged with compiling a "War Book" listing local assets, arrangements and responsibilities in accordance with a standard format issued by the Ministry of Home Security. In 1955 Lympstone's War Book, hand-written and bound with binder twine, was lodged with the Rector for safe keeping by Captain Young, the former Commander of the HG Platoon. Many years later it was saved from a bonfire by the late Ron Doidge and passed to the writer. In 1993, it was copied by the Imperial War Museum, bringing the total number of War Books in its possession to three.

Following a Lympstone Society Exhibition of old records and photographs in 1987, efforts were made to form a collection of Lympstone military activities, since when personal war-time reminiscences of many born or making their homes in Lympstone have been collected. This now constitutes an archive housed in eight lever arch files. Where possible, these accounts have been filed in chronological order enabling the reader, for instance, to note such facts as three Lympstonian Bomber Pilots being over Berlin on the night of 22nd November, 1943.

Ian Angus

A Lympstone VE Day celebration

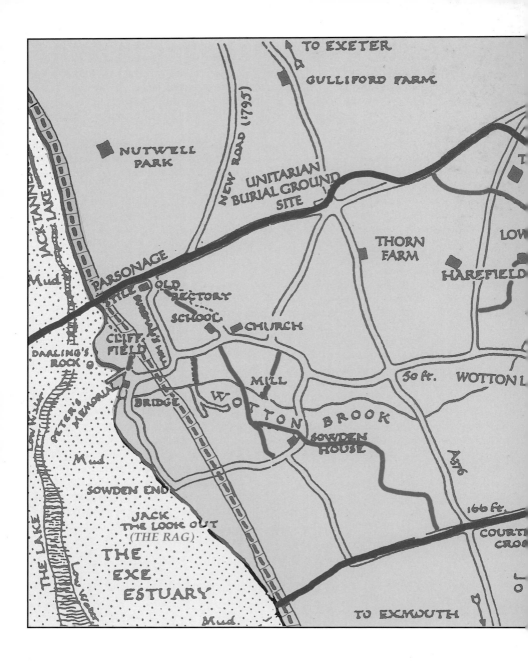

The Lympstone Parish Map

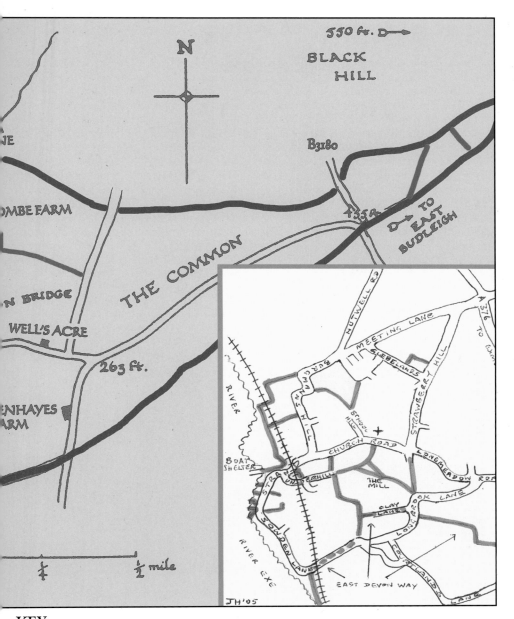

550 ft. ➤

BLACK HILL

B3180

TO EAST BUDLEIGH

THE COMMON

OMBE FARM

N BRIDGE

WELL'S ACRE

263 ft.

ENHAYES ARM

NUTWELL RD

MEETING LANE

A 376

TO EX

BURNTHOUSE HILL

GLEBELANDS

STRAWBERRY HILL

SCHOOL HILL

CHURCH ROAD

LONGMEADOW ROA

RIVER

BOAT SHELTER

STRAND

UNDERHILL

THE MILL

LONGBROOK LANE

CLAY LANE

COURTLANDS LANE

SOWDEN LANE

RIVER EXE

EAST DEVON WAY

JH '05

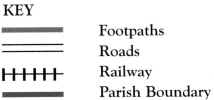

¼

½ mile

THE CHURCH

The dedication of the Parish Church of the Nativity of the Blessed Virgin Mary is unusual in England, thought to be unique, though in medieval times and nowadays in Roman Catholic parts of Europe it is well-known.

The church was consecrated by Bishop Edmund de Stafford on 24th September, 1409, after being re-built. However, the church goes far further back than 1409. There has been a Christian place of worship on this hill for nine hundred years or more. There is a strong tradition in the village of a Saxon church, but there is no architectural (or other) proof of this, Saxon churches being mostly built of wood which perishes. What does remain to us of earlier times is the stone Font bowl, rough-hewn with an axe in a cable-moulding typical of Norman work. It is thought by most experts indeed to be Norman. A Mr. Davidson, visiting in 1840, recounted that it had a stone pillar. This was lost at the reconstruction of the church in 1864, being turned out with the bowl to be used as a flower container! Fortunately, the bowl was not entirely lost, being rescued and brought inside to serve as a link with the early place of worship.

From various documentary records, we can go back as far as the 13th century, even as far as the 12th, since the Rector of 1329 requested Bishop de Grandisson to postpone consecration of the building because only parts of it were new. There was therefore another, earlier building in situ, which take us back to the 13th century at least. (Many

Parish Church of the Nativity of the Blessed Virgin Mary in Lympstone

churches were being built in the 12th and 13th centuries and parishes being organized.) Of the Norman records, the earliest date of a document referring to the church is 1228, when the Lord of the Manor, Reginald de Albemarle, gave his daughter and her husband some land by the Mill and the advowson of Lympstone church (this was the right to select and appoint the Rector, thus implying an existing church then). This would also imply a church which had been built earlier, in the 12th century, and was becoming decrepit through age. In 1251, Reginald created the Rectorial Manor of Lympstone, giving the right to the Rectors to hold a Manorial Court, and collect fines or rents from their Glebe land. This was only wound up, I believe, in the 20th century! Then in 1275 we have a record of a Rector, Henry dictus Potel, instituted by William de Albemarle, Lord of the Manor. By 1409, we have a record of a newly built church, complete with tower, consecrated the day after St. Swithun's church and new tower at Woodbury by Bishop Stafford on 23rd September. There is an obvious connection here. It comes in the form of the de Albemarle daughter who inherited both Lympstone and Woodbury and took them after her marriage to her husband, William de Bonville of Shute (d.1408). She was patron of both Lympstone and Woodbury churches. We know she gave Woodbury its church tower then. Was she thinking of her salvation and giving Lympstone not only its tower, but a new church too? Of this church the tower, built in the new Perpendicular style, remains, built partially of re-used material from earlier times, and also stone from a nearby quarry by the mill. Rough adze marks can be seen on the stones. In the interior, apart from the tower, three of the north aisle arches and the chancel arch remain from the medieval church of 1409. This church's north aisle is where later the tombs of the Drakes originally lay. If you look carefully, on the furthest left foliated capital by the chancel arch, you can see a medieval little Green Man!

The rest of the church is a Victorian reconstruction by a local architect, Mr. E. Ashworth: this was undertaken as the old church was so dilapidated. (Nevertheless, the Beer stone used by the 1409 builders has lasted much longer and better than the Bath stone used by the Victorians!) Apparently according to the Revd J.L. Fulford, who came from Woodbury to witness the demolition in 1863, the old church was 'all glorious within'. It was very rich in colour, with mural and roof decoration. The wall-plates of the nave and the north aisle were all painted vermilion and dull blue. The piers of the north arcade were banded with diagonal lines, alternately vermilion and emerald green, with intermediate mouldings in red. Throughout the nave and north aisle there was a very unusual pattern of yellow and emerald green. Also in the north aisle there was a mural of St. Christopher bearing the Holy Child, painted on a beautiful diaper ground. Finally, there was a rood loft and rood loft stairs. This all went.

The interior architecture of the church now looks neat and well-kept but somewhat unpromising. In Nikolaus Pevsner's words, it is 'conscientious but dull'. However, if you look well, there are treasures to find. There are many important features to discuss about the church, and those interested should consult the aforementioned *A Short History and Guide to Lympstone Parish Church*, by Rosemary Smith, 2002, available in the Lympstone Post Office; and Rosemary Burton's *Lympstone Parish Church* in the West Country Studies Library, Exeter. Rosemary Smith is indebted to articles by Mr. Davidson, 1840, and to books and articles by the Revd Gordon Browne, 1909, Beatrice F. Cresswell, 1920, Miss Dorothy Burton, Mrs. Elizabeth Scott, 1956, and to Mrs. Insull, 1964.

Rosemary Smith, M.A.

GULLIFORD

The Forgotten Chapel

An oil painting 1744 of the second Chapel at Gulliford

As I sit contemplating what angle to write this chapter from the thought occurred - I wonder how many Lympstone villagers have ever stepped through the Gulliford gates, how many even know it's there? Every schoolboy history textbook taught us of the danger in Tudor times of the constant swinging from Catholic faith to Protestant and how, if wishing to avoid a burning at the stake, it was safer to have a flexible attitude to religion. However, it was Cromwell's Puritans who allowed Nonconformists to flourish; that was until Charles II with his leaning back towards the Catholic church. In 1662 "The Act of Uniformity" tried to bring the clergy back in line, something which Samuel Fones, vicar of Woodbury, was unable to accept, costing him his livelihood with ten children to support. Dissenters were sent underground, but by William and Mary's reign a tenth of the population were Nonconformists and the "Toleration Act" of 1690 gave freedom to worship 'as long as it was not behind locked doors'. In the meantime, Samuel's loyal Presbyterian supporters were in need of a permanent location for which Thomas Lee of Sparkshayes donated a corner of his field (O.S. grid ref. SX996 847), situated in Meeting Lane (originally Chapel Lane), next to Boundary Cottage, opposite the turning to Strawberry Hill. The first chapel was erected in 1689, and by 1715 the congregation numbered five hundred! A second larger chapel replaced the original in 1744 having been built behind the first chapel on land paid for by Thomas Clarke (a painting of this chapel survives in Exmouth Library and can be viewed on request). The chapel continued to be popular with the congregation travelling miles, with between twelve and thirteen carriages often parked outside. The chapel offered two hundred and fifty free sittings and twenty others in 1755, with a private pew costing twenty shillings. Records for Gulliford are well documented and found at the Devon Record Office. Baptisms record known village names; Taylor, Teed, Shears, Upcott and Payne to mention but a few. In 1786 Richard Venman was paid £1.9s.1½d. for lime and reed and later in 1790, £1.5s.8d. for masonry work.

At some stage the chapel became Unitarian with the 1808 trustees including the Revd John Jervis, minister for Gulliford, Charles Baring (of the banking family) and Thomas Smith, gent. Investments were made to finance the chapel and ministers, namely £532.19s.3d. of South Sea Stock. Gulliford was not the only Nonconformist chapel around by now, as Exmouth saw the building of Lady Glenorchy's Chapel, resulting in a loss of donations.

By 1820 another chapel was built, this time in Lympstone village on the site of the present-day Ellenthorpe (grid ref. SX992 842). The Revd John Jervis oversaw its construction but died a fortnight before its opening service. However, the next minister proved unpopular and the congregation rapidly declined. By 1860 it was let to the Primitive Methodists and in 1887 (the Methodists now having built their own chapel), the chapel and land was sold off. As of yet, no records are known to have survived, including baptisms, marriages and burials, nor of its architecture.

In 1851 there was one regular Sunday service in the mornings at Gulliford with evening services in summer months only (although only 27 persons are shown to have attended the morning services). From the start it was decided that Gulliford chapel must not be used as a burying place for the dead: all burials were to be interred in the graveyard surrounding the chapel (on grounds of hygiene). In 1853 the following charges were announced: burials, common grave 10s.6d., minister's fee £1.1s., clerk and sexton 2s.6d. each or more up-market tomb with or without rail fence, £3.3s. Baptisms, minister's fee 1s., clerk and sexton 9d. each. Marriages, minister 10s. 6d., clerk and sexton 2s. each.

Gulliford Dissenters' Cemetery before grant aid for its restoration

Headstones mark the passing of Worthington Brice, Thomas Smith, the Barings and the Revd John Jervis - 'the faithfull, diligent and affectionate pastor of the congregation of Protestant Dissenters in this place, during the space of forty seven years ...', with many more lying hidden behind the ivy.

In 1887 the attendance was down to an average of ten; with the chapel having to fund itself it was existing on endowments. This was not helped by Mr. Sutherland, the minister, who without notice would cancel services much to the annoyance of what was left of the congregation. In his defence he was asked about it by the Trustees who accepted Mr. Sutherland's resignation, with the minister dying soon afterward.

By 1889 things had gone from bad to worse. The Trustees approached the Western Unitarian Christian Union with the view 'of disposal of the building and funds'. This was turned down. The linhay was demolished in 1899 and repairs were neglected; the roof was unsafe, the chapel walls needed strengthening and in 1907 Mr. Venman, the builder, was paid £20.7s. to pull the chapel down.

Today, Gulliford has passed into the hands of Woodbury and Lympstone Parish Councils and the graveyard is open to all. The perimeter wall and three tomb chest graves of Jervis, Lee and Stogdon are now listed, standing quietly behind the wooden gates shaded by overgrown yew and laurel, belonging to a time now past and forgotten.

Angela Coles

THE NATURAL ENVIRONMENT

Lympstone enjoys the best of three environmental worlds. Firstly, Lower Lympstone has river and sea combining in a mile-wide estuary, with glorious views across to the Powderham Estate lands on the opposite bank, extending to Dawlish Warren down river and up river to Exeter and the Cathedral. Sunsets here are magnificent as are the ever-changing aspects of light and water, varying from summer to winter - boats to birds. One can walk along the foreshore and footpath beside the railway to Exmouth - 'down to the mighty sea' - or wander up to Topsham and explore 'up the lazy river'. Climate change may create possible flooding problems from rising sea levels, and the Environment Agency is, at the time of writing (2005), working towards a Flood Prevention Scheme. Erosion of the red breccia cliffs is slow but regular; Darling Rock is shrinking before our eyes and the tree on the tip of the Cliff Field beside the little harbour is surely in jeopardy. However, slow change is inevitable and Lower Lympstone's charm will surely not be too compromised by this.

Secondly, Upper Lympstone has rich farmland and had orchards galore in times past. Although encroaching housing has reduced much of the farmland and more is threatened, there are still many fields and open spaces within the village which lift the spirit and make walking through the extensive network of footpaths a very pleasing experience. These footpaths almost certainly developed from routes used by villagers to get to the mill (for their flour), to the riverside (for their fish), to the church and to the

A view of Lympstone harbour

school, with inter-linking paths worn by many feet for convenience, not to mention the lack of mechanical transport!

Thirdly, beyond the main built-up village, and further emphasising its diversity, the parish boundary extends eastwards to Lympstone (and Woodbury) Commons, an area now recognized as extremely important pebble-bed heathland, being managed and controlled. This north-eastern tip of the parish is included within the East Devon Area of Outstanding Natural Beauty (AONB), making Lympstone one of 29 parishes in and around this special area.* It is great walking country and affords marvellous views towards Sidmouth's Peak Hill and the sea to the east as well as to the estuary, the Haldon Hills and Dartmoor to the west.

Lympstone has a tremendous advantage in that the cliffs at either end of the "bay" have restricted development: the National-Trust-owned Cliff Field to the north and the rising cliffs towards Sowden End to the south create a "contained" waterfront with no opportunity for "seaside sprawl". Beyond these cliffs, two estates, Nutwell and Courtlands, are worthy of note since they have preserved extensive green spaces at either end of the village. Although neither is normally open to the public, Nutwell Court (leased around 1721 and then purchased in 1802 by Sir Francis Drake's family) with its different styles of architecture and its chapel, the beautiful lake close to the house graced by black swans, and the surrounding land may be explored when public events are being held there. The Courtlands estate is crossed when "Beating the Bounds" takes place every four or five years, but also the house and grounds are more accessible now, since it has become a venue for events and weddings. This estate abuts Lower Halsdon Farm, generously bequeathed to the National Trust in 2002 by the Long family, which provides a vital environmental green space to separate Lympstone from Exmouth and so retain its identity. This significant gesture was marked by the installation of a Blue Plaque, a joint enterprise between the Exmouth Society and The Lympstone Society in 2003.

All this of course has meant that Lower Lympstone expanded eastwards to meet Upper Lympstone and now we have a delightfully varied and integrated village, closely linked by the charming Wotton Brook flowing throughout and also linked by the situation, roughly in the centre, of the parish church, village hall and school. There is a wide diversity of housing, and this creates a viable and thriving village in terms of population - children for the school, patients for the doctors' surgery and customers for the Post Office and the village shop and hostelries.

* *The East Devon AONB was designated in 1963 to conserve and enhance this attractive landscape. The AONB Partnership is a joint initiative working with a broad range of authorities and local groups to secure a living, working landscape. For more information about the AONB, visit www.eastdevonaonb.org.uk*

The creation of a Village Design Statement (in 2004) is a positive step towards maintaining the environmental attractiveness of the village. Progress is necessary, as are jobs and homes, especially affordable housing, but the VDS should ensure that in future these can be achieved without spoiling the character of the village - it's not what you do but the way that you do it!

Blue Plaque at Lower Halsdon Farm with the Chairmen of the Lympstone and Exmouth Societies and of the National Trust Regional Committee

The *natural* environment is a major aspect of pleasurable living, and our village has a goodly share of hedgerows and banks sporting lots of wild bushes and flowers - a joy in spring. Tree cover is extensive, with a profusion of evergreen holm oaks, notably all around the Cliff Field, and a wealth of other mature trees of all kinds for us to value, sparing an appreciative thought for our forbears who planted for future generations. Although, sadly, cider production has ceased, there are some very productive garden orchards remaining, and even small gardens in the village have a profusion of trees and shrubs. Lympstone and the estuary are protected from the worst weather by Dartmoor and the Haldon Hills with storms often passing to the west and north of these, and thus the village enjoys a mild climate conducive to a profusion of plants and flowers. Having been a 'Britain in Bloom' winner in 1985, the village prides itself still on producing an abundant wealth of colour through window boxes, hanging baskets, tubs and gardens, a joy to behold every summer. The effect is delightful and is very much appreciated by visitors and residents alike.

So much for Flora - what of Fauna? The more rural parts of the village support the usual mammals such as rabbits, foxes, badgers (particularly in the Wotton Valley), grey squirrels, hedgehogs and, less noticeably, stoats and weasels, fieldmice and voles. However, increasing traffic and consequent pollution, the grubbing-up of hedges, tree-felling and verge-cutting have all contributed to a reduction in habitat and therefore a sad decline in animal population. This trend may be partly reversed by the (2004) intention of the government to implement conditions set by the EU for farmers' subsidies, namely to ban hedge cutting between March and July and to increase wildlife habitat alongside hedges, ditches and watercourses. On the heathlands, there are deer a-plenty and the excellent management of these heaths may, hopefully, lead to numbers of other species rising again. The estuary is home to a vast wealth of birds, both resident and migratory, and the rest of the village and commons have their fair share of other bird species *(please see next chapter)*. According to a 2004 report, farmland birds as well as urban birds are in decline not only in Britain, but across Europe. However, it has also been reported that new species are appearing here (from warmer climates - through global warming?). Nature is obviously adapting; our natural environment may change, but not too much, we hope!

People who were born in Lympstone mostly wish to stay, or return; many others have chosen to come to live here. I'm sure that a major reason for this is that Lympstone's environment is special and precious - and long may it remain so.

Julie Horwood

BIRD LIFE

Exe Estuary

This is one of the major estuaries of the south-west and is of national and international importance for wintering waders and wildfowl. These come to take advantage of the rich food supply present in the sand and mud of the river bed. Of wintering waders, dunlin are usually present in hundreds, together with large numbers of redshank and flocks of fifty or more black-tailed godwit. Smaller numbers of turnstone, ringed plover and grey plover can be seen. Little egrets are now a common sight, whilst the graceful greenshank sometimes visits the lower part of the estuary. The number of wintering avocets is increasing every year and they can often be seen at low tide from the Goat Walk in Topsham.

Of wintering wildfowl, brent geese, wigeon and teal are present in their hundreds, with smaller numbers of pintail, goldeneye, merganser, great-crested and little grebe. Curlew and oystercatcher are present most of the year, often in large numbers; their characteristic calls are a familiar sound. Mallard, shelduck and Canada geese (originally escapees from private wildfowl collections) are numerous at various times of the year. Herons are a familiar sight; the heronry where they breed is on the Powderham estate. Cormorants, in heraldic pose, are also a common sight on the sandbanks. An osprey can sometimes be seen fishing during migration and a peregrine falcon surveying large flocks from a great height, searching for an unwary straggler.

The acquisition by the RSPB of the flooded fields at Bowling Green Marsh, Topsham, has encouraged more winter visitors to the area. Flocks of 2,000 wigeon, 1,100 black-tailed godwit and 800 teal were recorded in 2004. During the spring and autumn migration many interesting species pass through and may stay for a short time. These include whimbrel, common sandpiper, curlew sandpiper, bar-tailed godwit, pochard, tufted duck and common and sandwich terns. Recent rarities in the area include scaup, lesser scaup and green-winged teal. Spoonbill and a single glossy ibis have been regular visitors in recent years.

Woodland, Field and Hedgerow

The common hedgerow birds, finches, tits (including long-tailed tits) etc. are well represented throughout the year and there are large rookeries present in the parish. Green and great spotted woodpeckers are present in wooded areas and are common visitors to gardens. The predators kestrel, sparrow hawk and buzzard are regularly seen. The peregrine hunts over this habitat as well as the river.

Summer migration brings several species of warbler including chiffchaff, blackcap, whitethroat and the rarer lesser whitethroat. Some chiffchaff and blackcap now stay in the area throughout the year. Swallows are now fewer in number in the area as are swifts. Fortunately, house martins seem to be keeping their numbers steady.

Redwing and fieldfare are becoming less common visitors now that we have milder winters. Lapwing are not seen in such large numbers as before when huge flocks were a common sight in local fields. Golden plover can still be seen in small numbers.

Common Land and Heath

Part of the parish includes common land which is also rich in bird life. In early morning or evening in fine summer weather it is still possible to hear the cuckoo. Stonechat, meadow pipit, and various warblers are present, including the rare Dartford warbler which is resident. At dusk the peculiar churring of the nightjar can be heard, perhaps with a sighting of its mysterious display flight. Another summer visitor occasionally seen is the attractive falcon the hobby, which preys on larger insects and birds such as swallows.

Geoff Hackston, kindly revised and updated by **Mary Nightingale**

FISHING

Past and Present

Salmon Fishermen - left to right: (Tiger) Harold Mitchell, Chris Squires, John Squires, Sam Squires

There are those still alive in Lympstone (2005) who remember that Lympstone Lake even 60 years ago was much bigger and came much further in to the shore. Nutwell, the Belvedere and Exton all had streams which helped to feed the river levels, as did the Wotton Brook which was much bigger and wider then. This would have been of enormous consequence to fishermen. Going further back to the late Middle Ages, there is evidence in the estuaries of the Teign, the Exe, the Otter and the Axe that, where once there had been thriving ports for fishing and the coastal trade (Topsham, Exeter, Ottermouth, Seaton) often well inland, silting up of the estuaries occurred. At some period shingle stopped up the mouths of the rivers. The Exe, for instance, once ran out at Langstone Cliff. This would have meant higher tides coming in, and it can be speculated that Lympstone might not have depended so much on tides for getting its boats out, not only for fishing, but for launching a boat built here.

Lympstone was an important port in the Middle Ages and later depended mainly on shipbuilding and the coastal trade for its living (together with farming). Ships built here went to Plymouth Dockyard to be finished in more recent times.

Shipbuilding, however, as we have seen, came to an end in the early nineteenth century, due to the size of boats required, the introduction of iron boatbuilding, and the coming of the railway. People then either went to Plymouth or Wales, etc., or turned to

The last big herring catch (note top right Jim Squires)

fishing here for a living. The coastal trade, in addition, stopped in October and did not begin again until the spring. Either way, of necessity, people turned to fishing: families with six to ten children had to find ways to feed them. Lympstone soon became one of the most important fishing ports in the region until well after the Second World War. Between 1920-80 there were 80 registered fishing boats here. After the First World War, fishermen put their gratuities into even bigger boats and there was a thriving trade. The coming of the railway in 1861 had opened up large markets, and in the early twentieth century buyers came from the Midlands to get fish and fish went up to Billingsgate too. There was a 3p.m. goods train up to London, or if you missed that, the 6p.m. passenger train would guarantee fish getting to Billingsgate market by 6a.m.

Lympstone people still remember the old mackerel boats that sailed from the village. They had names such as "Never Despair", "Onward", "Advance", "True Blue" and "Trump". They were open boats, but designed and rigged on the lines of the better-known Brixham trawlers, though only half the length. Because they did not have the necessary weight and sail area, they normally used lines rather than trawls. Times changed with the arrival of engines, and drift-netting took the place of line fishing. Drift nets have diamond-shaped openings of such size that the fish are caught by the gills. The nets, supported at the head by floats and weighted at the foot so that they hung vertically, were shot at right-angles to the expected route of the fish. It is highly skilled work depending on knowledge of the habits of the fish and observation of their whereabouts at particular times. Now, of course, the heavy mackerel fishing by great trawlers has finished this trade in Lympstone.

The village used to have a very prosperous shellfish trade which other ports did not, and this used to be very important in the winter. At one time over 2,000 bags a week went out of the village - mostly mussels. However in the 1920s cases of food poisoning put down to shellfish caused the authorities to specify one week's purifying in tanks at

Salmon crew treating nets c. 1930

Sowden End. This brought an end to the trade, for after carrying by horse and cart before and after purifying, the mussels were not viable. Pollution of the river also finished the sale of mussels in Lympstone. There are often large numbers of cockles and mussels inside the estuary, though the numbers vary from year to year. Some time ago there was a huge 'spat' of mussels on Lympstone ridge, but these were taken in very large numbers and not many now remain. 'Snips' Stamp used to say mussels were good until 14th March and that winkles could be an early morning job, depending on the tide. He raised winkles on the 'Klondike' bank, which took 6-18 months to fatten.

There was also a very successful trade in salmon fishing in the early 20th century. The biggest recorded haul was in 1930 when 108 were taken on one tide, and old photographs exist showing salmon by the cartload. The Exe Board of Conservators and the National

1910 - Making a haul to pull in the salmon

19th century photograph of fishermen mending their nets. Note the bowlers and the sailor.

Neil Binmore, Jason and Ambrose Ingham

Rivers Authority, however, stopped the traditional ways of salmon fishing, that is by a moving net, and specified a static net. This, together with heavy licensing, and the later competition with fish farming, meant trade went down. The last salmon fishing consisted of two boats out in 1988. Topsham may still have some.

As to herring fishing, there is a sad tale of decline here too. After herring had begun to return to the area in the 1980s, and big catches had been landed at the harbour, the Ministry, following E.E.C. conservation rules, placed a ban on all herring fishing in 1983. Big trawlers were then allowed to dredge for scallops on the herring breeding grounds, which broke up the coral bed in Lyme Bay and off Budleigh; thus both herring and scallop breeding grounds (the same) were destroyed at one fell swoop.

There are no more fishermen making their living by fishing left in Lympstone but there is fishing by rod and line from open boats - usually anchored above or close to the main channel - or even from the harbour wall. Fish commonly caught are plaice, dabs and flounders. Mackerel, too, can be caught by spinners towed behind moving boats. Visitors anxious to try their luck would be wise first to ask local retired or part-time fishermen for their advice.

Norman Mitchell and David Burton with Edgar Norton

Storm coming up over the river

FARMING

Haymaking in the 1920s

'Devon is ... predominantly an agricultural county, and is the product of more than 50 generations of farmers cultivating the land' - so says John Lane in his book *In Praise of Devon*. However, he also says that by far the greater part of Devon's population is urban (in 1998). About 600,000 out of 1,049,000 people live in Exeter, Plymouth and Torbay.

About two-thirds of the county's farms existed before 1066, and most are of the greatest antiquity. Medieval farming expanded through the 12th-14th centuries, with the greatest peak before the Black Death (1348), which wiped out nearly half the population and caused decline in agriculture. In the 16th and 17th centuries, there was measured prosperity, seen in the tax assessments and the re-building of many Devon farmsteads, dating from 1560-1640. Two hundred years later, there were falling returns and also ups and downs in returns. For instance, there was agricultural prosperity during the war of 1793-1815, then the exact opposite in the peace which came after. Cheap American and Canadian corn in the late 1870s and 1880s brought about a disastrous price-fall for English corn, which earlier had suffered from bad harvests. 19th century industrialisation meant farm workers and their families often migrated to towns, and there was migration too from Lympstone to America and Canada as well as other parts of England.

Farming has always been part of traditional economic activity in Lympstone. E.A.G. Clark says: 'Lympstone has been both fishing village and agricultural settlement...' Small farms existed throughout the village in medieval times, and later were concentrated in Upper Lympstone. (Fishing and boat-building were of course

The Hayman Family, Lower Coombe Farm front garden:
John Hayman, Sylvia Hayman, Lily Hayman. Mary Hayman, Tom Hayman
Fred Hayman, Grandma Hayman, Samuel Hayman, Richard Hayman

economic activities in Lower Lympstone.) The large estate of Nutwell Court owned tracts of land which, under the Drakes and long before, under the de Dynhams, were continuously farmed. The Peters' estate had been farmed long before the Peters arrived in the 19th century. The Courtlands estate is also extensive farming land, though Courtlands itself is just over the parish boundary in Exmouth. Gulliford Farm belonged to the Drake estate from 1800-1941, though strictly outside Lympstone parish, and was farmed from 1820-1991 by the Hallett family, who bought Gulliford outright in 1941. In 1991 they sold it. Part of the estate was compulsorily purchased by the Admiralty just before the war for the new Commando Training Centre.

Farming around the date of the Tithe Map (1839) is described in Professor Kain's chapter on *Geographical Continuity and Change* (see page 3). Farms were smaller, more numerous, with more mixed farming, sheep, horses and many more orchards. There were then the following farms: Backenhayes, Burnthouse, Exe View, Goodmores, Harefield, Hills, Linhayes, Lower Coombe, Lympstone House, Marley Lodge, Middle Coombe, Nutts, Pitt Farm, Potter's Farm, Sowden Farm (part), Sowden (part), Sowden House, Strawberry Hill, Thorn Farm, Wotton Farm, Wotton Bridge and Wootton Farm - twenty two farms in all.

In the 20th century, Backenhayes, Burnthouse, Goodmores, Linhayes, Potter's, Sowden Farm, Town Dairy and Underhill were all lost as farms and many others were turned into market gardens.

Agricultural methods have changed greatly. Mr. Wilfred Bailey has described a typical day of a farmer in the 1920s. The farmer's day began at 5.30a.m. with milking the cows by hand, which finished only about 7a.m., as there were 25-30 cows to milk. The milk was then taken by pony and trap to Mr. White's Dairies in Exmouth. The farmer and his wife and two men worked the farm. The two men were paid 37s.6d. a week. There were normally six carthorses and a pony on the farm as well as the cows. The work was particularly hard in the winter, with ploughing in the rain, hedges to be cut and laid by hand, and turfing up the drains. Wells often had to be dug 60ft. deep. The farmer's day did not end until late in the evening in summer, though at dark in the winter.

Nowadays, farming has been greatly mechanised, with tractors instead of horses, and milking machines doing the milking quicker. Some farms have been amalgamated to give bigger acreage, and larger fields formed. Oil seed rape has made an appearance in fields under plough.

Four generations of Baileys have farmed in Lympstone. Mr. Bailey's great-grandfather, John, farmed at Pitt Farm in the 1890s. Mr. Bailey's father, Walter Bailey, farmed at Thorn Farm, and Wilfred Bailey was born there. He farmed Thorn Farm from 1937-1981, after his brother James in the early 1930s. In 2005, Mr. Jim Bailey farms at Lower Coombe Farm and Mr. Trevor Bailey at Thorn Farm, Lympstone.

Mr. Wilfred Bailey remembers that farm land used to sell at £20 an acre in the 1930s. He also remembers a market in Lympstone at the Saddlers' Arms, held every fortnight by Hussey's, the auctioneers, selling cattle, pigs and other farm produce.

In spite of E.U. regulations and the Common Agricultural Policy, it is to be hoped that farming will prosper more locally in the future, and that the politicians will come to recognize its importance.

Rosemary Smith, M.A.

The Boat Shelter, Lympstone

THE RAILWAY

The Line to Lympstone

Lympstone Railway Station 1904

1.p.m. The Artillery Band strikes up the march and the procession moves off. It is the 1st May, 1861, the opening day of the Exeter and Exmouth Railway in Exmouth. The procession leaves The Parade and heads up North Street across The Beacon before returning to the station. The Artillery Band is followed by The Volunteer Rifles, Exmouth Brass Band, the Directors of the Railway, tradesmen, local children and finally the children from the Ragged School.

Trains had been arriving at Exeter from 1st May, 1844 from Bristol, with the South Devon Railway going westwards from 30th May, 1844.

The branch line had been a long time in coming. Plans had been put foward in 1845 by both the Exeter and Exmouth Railway and Exeter, Topsham and Exmouth Railway, including a plan of 1854 to lay the tracks out of Exeter towards Exminster, crossing the canal and the River Exe before reaching Exmouth.

The chosen route led from Exeter Queen Street (Central), Lions Holt Halt (St. James' Park), through Black Boy Tunnel, Mount Pleasant Road Halt, Exmouth Junction (with its own staff and engine shed), the sidings to the brick and chemical works, Polsloe Bridge Halt, Clyst St. Mary and Digby Halt (with a siding off to Digby Mental Hospital), sidings into the United States and UK Naval Depot, Newcourt Depot, Topsham (with a line down Holman Way to the Quay), siding into Odam's Fertiliser Factory, Woodbury Road (Exton), Lympstone Commando, Lympstone (Village), Warren's Siding into the East Devon Brick and Tile Co., Exmouth and finally down to the Exmouth Dock complete with turntable.

Lympstone, formerly London and South Western, later Southern Railway, had a platform of 323ft., with the original signal box opposite the southern end of the platform; this was replaced in 1929 with a signal box on the south side of the booking office. The station buildings consisted of a booking hall, general waiting room, ladies' room, toilets, parcel shed and, on the platform, chocolate and chewing gum slot machines, a weighing machine and First Aid cupboard.

Double-headed 82-0XX BR standard class 3MT tank engines at Lympstone between 1952 and 1963. The last steam passenger timetable service was in 1963; freight trains continued until 1965. The last steam passenger tour train ran in 1994.

To the north, a single arched brick footbridge and at Parsonage Stile a metal footbridge cross the line, while just south of the station, a three-arched viaduct takes the railway over The Strand. There was a goods line with a short siding towards the north with a cattle dock; also a siding in the Cliff Field cutting and allotments alongside the track.

Freight consisted of milk churns, shellfish, crabs, mail, coal, parcels and morning and evening newspapers. The single line north and south of Lympstone was controlled by a Tyer no. 6 tablet workings, with the goods yard closing in April, 1960 and the signal box finishing in September, 1962.

At the Exmouth end of the platform was a foot-crossing to the first signal box and beyond a gate into the station master's house, Dalkeith (now Queen Anne House). In 1891 railway employees in Lympstone included John Tolman, platelayer, William Clarke, signalman and Irishman Edward Jenkins acting as porter. Other railwaymen working at Lympstone station included: signalman Mr. Allen, Ernie Prew, Jack Gosney, George Reynolds, Sid Knight, Tom Luscombe, Reg Salway, Peter Fry, Peter Wole (clerk), Frank Love, with the last station master Mr. Veale.

On 20th August, 1964, it was announced that the Exeter and Exmouth line had escaped Dr. Beeching's proposed cuts, though Budleigh Salterton and Sidmouth fared differently.

Today's sprinter trains take the place of the M7 steam trains and more recently, the diesel DMUs, with the odd special putting in an appearance, for example a 125 HST in 1996 down from Birmingham to Exmouth for the naming of the lifeboat. Since the disbanding of British Railways the branch line has witnessed the names Regional Railways, Wales and West, and Wessex, but basically the network remains the same although the station is a ghost of its former self, with a shelter, one-way information speaker, waste bin and two outside benches.

The Railway Hotel has become the Swan Inn. Tickets are now bought from the guard on the train, whereas in the past in the cold weather, after purchasing your ticket in the ticket office you would retire to the waiting room to warm yourself by the fire kept stoked by the platform staff.

The writer wishes to thank Messrs. Robert Perry, Bill Smith, Peter Fry and Robin Coles for sharing their information and memories.

Angela Coles

SCHOOLING

The Beginnings

The beginnings of schooling in Lympstone were due to private benefactors, and their endowments went mainly to Sunday Schools. There is a record of Captain Metherell leaving £4 rent-charge to schooling by his Will of 1727, and of an Egerton legacy of £1 per annum in 1730. However, it is in the Rectors' *Returns to Visitation Queries* of 1798 that mention is first made of 'two or three small schools for young children', and in 1818 the Return records two small dame schools for six and four children.

One such dame school was that run at Romany Cottage in the early 1820s or 1830s, the cottage then being owned by the Longs. A relation of theirs, a Miss Langdon, had a small school there for some years.

Another example was the dame school at Brook Cottage, originally a farm, and one house then. A Mrs. Fidler and her husband had several daughters to educate and lived at Brook Cottage. They had the idea of founding a school for other people's daughters too and to educate them all. "A School for Young Ladies" was opened and Rosemary Burton has written that there was 'special attention paid to Morals, Health and Manners, Ladies under ten £22 per annum, Ladies over ten £26 per annum'.

It was in 1823, however, that provision for a public day school appears to have been begun by Elizabeth Welch, the widow of Wakelyn Welch, Esq., who built and endowed the original school in her husband's memory. The school was founded for religious teaching, the three "R"s and fine sewing. At first this school was the Boys' School, called the Boys' National School only in 1841, when a Mr. Ebbels was appointed Boys' Master at £30 per annum. He also probably became the teacher of the Sunday School as well. At this time, there appears to be a first government grant coming to the schools. Before this, from 1818, the Sunday Schools for 24 boys and 26 girls were supported by subscription and the Welch bequest of £2.13s.4d. per annum.

It was not until 1844 that Mrs. Harriet Feasey Wyatt gave £1,000 'to be annually applied to the instruction of poor girls in the principles of the Church of England and Elementary Secular subjects; also for providing a Schoolmistress her wages'. White's Directory of 1850 reports that the Girls' Mistress received £24 per annum from Mrs. Harriet Feasey Wyatt, which points to the Girls' School being entirely supported by a private patron. From the Directories, it seems that the Girls' School was called "Free School" until at least 1873, while the name "National" was confined then to the Boys' School. In 1876-77, however, the management of both was amalgamated and the term "National" probably applied to both.

CHARITIES

HARRIETT FEESEY WYATT IN THE YEAR 1844 GAVE £1000 TO BE ANNUALLY APPLIED TO THE INSTRUCTION OF POOR GIRLS IN THE PRINCIPLES OF THE CHURCH OF ENGLAND AND ELEMENTARY SECULAR SUBJECTS; ALSO FOR PROVIDING A SCHOOLMISTRESS

Extra subscriptions, after two appeals, provided a rise to £40 per annum for the Boys' School Master in 1851, and in 1853 the Government offered a capitation grant for boys who attended at least 176 days in a year. This, however, brought in little, for the attendance was too irregular to qualify. In 1858 there came a small book grant of £2.6s.0d. and increased expenditure at the school.

However this was not met by Government grant as yet. There was deficit and financial crisis in 1860. By 1867, however, Government grant was now sufficient, with other sources, to provide a small surplus. This was in spite of a new floor in the Boys' schoolroom which cost £17!

The Establishment of Public Education

Then in 1870 came the famous Education Act, which made the Government responsible for education for all. Having found that the Boys' and Girls' Schools had between them room for 86 scholars, the managers now had to provide for double that number. In 1871 there were open fires in the boys' and girls' rooms, with coal, not coke, as fuel. In that year, there were still only two teachers for the girls, Mrs. Mary Ann Long and Miss Winsor from Exmouth. In 1872, a new wing was built on to the Girls' School which cost £370. This sum was raised by voluntary subscriptions. However the Girls' School was still a separate institution under an uncertificated teacher, and it was felt that it should be put on a more recognized footing. So in 1876-77 the management of both schools came under a Committee composed of the Rector, the Churchwardens and six other supporters. This meant that the finances came under the Voluntary Rate, and allowed the appointment of a certificated Mistress to make the Girls' School grant-earning. The grant was vastly increased in the 1890s and the finances were much improved. Finally, the school was taken over by the County in 1903, when the total salary bill was found to be £319.4s.0d. or £2.12s.10d. per head, which was apparently very generous for Devon at that time.

The various teachers at the school in the 19th century and their salaries are detailed by the late Dr. Sellman, who conducted an Exeter University Extra-Mural class in Lympstone, on aspects of Lympstone, in 1973. Another source is the *Pupils' Book*: in this, Mrs. Newton in Chapter 1 says: 'The period from 1877 on was, I suppose, very hard times. The Master always kept a cane on his desk, and if anyone whispered one word, he caned them'. The hours at school were 9a.m. to 12.15, and 1.30 to 4p.m.

Two of the last teachers of the 19th century at the school were Mr. and Mrs. Sheppard (who lived at Fairview, now Sheppard's on Church Road). The era of the Sheppards lasted through the First World War right up to 1920 when, exhausted, they both retired. She ran the Girls' School, according to Mr. Stamp, in a separate building from the Boys', and he was Headmaster who taught at the Boys', helped by one pupil-teacher. The late Mr. Litton remembers that when he was a small boy, the late Miss Topsy Reynolds, a lacemaker in the village, was the knitting teacher for infants in the Boys' School, and recalls she was about three months older than he was!

During the Sheppards' time, the school became the Public Elementary School Mixed Infants. In 1920 Francis Albert King, who had arrived at the school in 1890, became Headmaster. In 1929 he is living at Ellenthorpe with his wife and family. In the 1920s, the school had coke stoves for heating and gas for lighting. The children did have a playground then (only recent) and they did P.T. in it. Mr. King continued until 1932, when Mr. Cloke became Headmaster. They still had gas lights in school, then acquired a gas cooker. By now the children had a bottle of milk every morning, for which they paid a halfpenny. There were still no school meals, far less a school bus, and some children had a very long way to walk. In 1933 the children got new locker desks. In the same year they started keeping poultry.

The Lympstone Primary School

MAYPOLE 1953

Barry James, Kenneth Morrish, Ivor Finn, Laurie Sansom, Michael Partridge, Neil Parsons, Michael Hodge, Kenneth Hall, Peter Perryman, Dodie Roe, Jennifer James, Valerie Pearcey, Fay Scagg, Marion Potter, Pamela Reading, Rosemary Land, Rosalind Dakin

In 1936 the school became the Junior School, and the older children went on to Exmouth. There were still about 40 in a class, and four classes. Heating was still by coke stove. Mr. Cloke remained until 1938; then came the war the next year.

During the war there were three classes, and evacuees came, but they were in Lympstone House and had classes there. The evacuees came down in batches, with their teachers. The Headmistress at first was Miss Parkinson, from 1938-1941, then Miss Flux, 1941-1943, and then came Mr. Hills who taught the boys in Lympstone House. School milk was issued, but charged for at a halfpenny a time. Towards the end of the war the teachers were: Miss Stark, with a class of 18, Mrs. Farley, with a class of 23, and Mrs. Bamsey.

In the post-war period, milk became free to pupils and school dinners were provided at 5d. each. Electricity was now put in, and there was a canteen in the Village Hall. The teachers were at first: Miss Sharland, Miss Addington and Mrs. Farley, and then Miss G. Musell, Miss Addington, Mrs. Farley and the Headmistress, Miss Stark.

From the 1960s to the 1980s there were many developments. A swimming pool was dug during which excavation a coin, a silver half-groat of Henry VII, was found *(see right)*. The swimming pool, however, was later filled in again. School meals are taken now in the Village Hall, the old canteen! And the last two Head Teachers, Gareth Thomas, 1986-1998, and Anthony Priest, January 1999 onwards, have been laying the foundations for their pupils to go forward in the 21th century.

There is a need for a School History to cover the years since the war up to the present time (2005) and it is hoped one will be forthcoming soon.

Rosemary Smith, M.A.

SOCIAL ACTIVITIES

There is a very wide range of social and sporting activities in Lympstone, remarkable in a village of its size (population now c.2,000; 1,884 at the 2001 Census).

There is a very popular Arts Group, which puts on a demonstration once a year in the spring with an annual exhibition in the summer. There is an active Boxing Club and Football Club, which arrange coaching, practices and matches. The Lympstone Amateur Boxing Club meet in Exmouth, train juniors on Tuesdays and Thursdays seniors on Mondays and women (only) on Wednesdays. There is a present possibility of a Cricket Club being formed. A thriving and popular Garden Club puts on an annual show with competitions in August. It also has a programme of talks. The very popular Lympstone Players put on frequent performances of exceedingly high standard (now often accompanied, cafe-style, by a delicious dinner). They also hold regular play and poetry readings in members' houses. The Lympstone South-West Telecoms Band, which has won many prestigious awards, practices twice a week and holds a training practice for new players on Saturdays to which they welcome beginners. They encourage younger members to come to learn an instrument which they will lend to them. By request of The Lympstone Society, they give a band concert in the church once a year, but constantly give concerts elsewhere. The Parish Church has an active Bellringing team and they welcome visitors to their Wednesday night practice. The Sailing Club, with its clubhouse at the Boat Shelter by the limekiln, holds many events during the season April-September. They also hold social evenings in the club. Sea-Scouts, Brownies, a Playgroup and a thriving Pre-School also feature in village life, with playgrounds being organised by Lympstone@play. The Tennis Club has very good all-weather courts beside the Village Hall and organizes matches and tennis coaching for all ages. Another important club is the Shop Supporters' Club. Lympstone was threatened with the closure of its local shop, but, owing to the efforts of a dedicated group, the local butcher and to funds loaned by local people, the Shop Supporters' Club was formed. This local shop has not only been kept open but goes from strength to strength. The Twinning Association arranges events and exchange visits with Bieville-Beuville in northern France. There is a very thriving Women's Institute in the village, which among their many activities, provide some helpers for the Wednesday Lunch Club. Last but not least, there is a Third Age Project, involving many senior citizens; and some specialist clubs, for example bridge and Curios Music Group.

The Village Hall, which is run by a Committee under the Parish Council, is the venue for the larger indoor or winter events. Now with a well-equipped Function Room at one end, the Village Hall welcomes bookings from local clubs and societies

Craning out, 1997

including the Players, the Church and The Lympstone Society. It has a monthly Social and runs the occasional dance. Instead of the old Youth Club, there is to be a new Society - the Lympstone Young People's Society - (from 2005), with an entirely refurbished building. For open-air events, the village owns Candy's Field and also has the use of Cliff Field and the adjoining Avenue Field, both of which belong to the National Trust (given by Miss Sheldon of the Manor House when she moved in 1940).

Furry Dance, Lympstone

Then there is the Furry Dance, a very popular event, held on the first Saturday in August. It is organized by a Committee together with the Lympstone S.W. Telecoms Band, who lead the fancy-dress dancers through the village from the Globe to the Saddlers' Arms and back again to the Swan, collecting for charity as they go. Reminiscent of Cornish custom, it is not known when this dance started.

Another event held every four or five years is Beating the Bounds, when the village turns out to follow the ancient Parish Boundary and to beat the old boundary stones. The numbers participating show the pride of villagers in their ancient parish.

Lympstone is also closely associated with the Royal Marines. The Commando Training Centre, Royal Marines is situated on the A376 past Nutwell; their quarters are in Lympstone Parish and and Marine families shop and mix in Lympstone while children swell the numbers at the Primary School.

The Church of England Primary School caters for about 110 children (in 2005) and is supported by an active PTFA which runs a variety of social events and gives financial support to the school. On a private level, there is a Language School being run in Lympstone, which adds to the mix of the community.

In all, there are at the time of writing in 2005, 36 associations, clubs, groups or organizations in Lympstone Village. Their activities are publicised in the unique village newspaper, *The Lympstone Herald*. A list of them with current contacts is held in the Post Office, or visit: www.Lympstone.org

Truly, everyone should be able to find an interest here!

Beating the Bounds

THE LYMPSTONE SOCIETY

The Lympstone Society is the conservation and amenity society of the village. Formed during Conservation Year, 1970, it is affiliated to the Civic Trust, The Campaign to Protect Rural England (C.P.R.E.), and to the Devon Conservation Forum. It has (in 2005) c.214 members. The Society has been given or lent valuable old records, maps, Indentures, Wills, pictures, photographs and some scrap-books. It actively welcomes any additions to preserve for posterity. Documents, Indentures and photographs can be photocopied and the

Outing to Cothay Manor and Gardens, Somerset, 2003

originals returned to their owners. Tape recordings have been and continue to be made of some of the older Lympstonians' and residents' tales of life in the village.

The Society arranges a mixed programme of meetings, visits, exhibitions, concerts, talks and lectures by experts on conservation, history, the wildlife habitat, geology, local government and other wide-ranging topics. Outings and visits by coach, car, train or boat are arranged to places of interest during the summer. Its publications include: *The Lympstone Story*, and this, its re-written successor; a leaflet: *A Visitor's Guide to Lympstone* - a short guide to what to see and do in the village by Angela Coles; *A Short History and Guide to the Church*, by Rosemary Smith. There is also a pictorial map, produced to celebrate the Millennium, which gives an illustrated history of Lympstone from the Bronze Age to the last World War. All of these are on sale at the Post Office.

The Lympstone Society hopes eventually to be able to store many of its documents of interest and the copy of its Tithe Map of 1839 in a central building in the village, with much easier access. At the moment, for reasons of security, they are stored in a private house, but can be consulted by arrangement. Please contact the Society through the Post Office. The Devon Record Office holds some documents, maps etc. which are not so often consulted, in their safe hands.

Rosemary Smith, M.A., Editor

The Editor wishes to thank particularly David Burton, a past Editor, for his advice, help and for his photographs; Rosemary Burton, a past Chairman, for her help and work; Iris Walker, now in Canada, who designed and painted the 'Millennium Map'; Julie Horwood, for her invaluable help with production and publication; and to all who have contributed articles, paintings, drawings, photographs or time to this new *Lympstone Story* and to the Society.

Outing to Plymouth and the harbour by boat, 2001